The Role of the Legal Information Officer

CHANDOS
INFORMATION PROFESSIONAL SERIES

Chandos' new series of books are aimed at the busy information professional. They have been specially commissioned to provide the reader with an authoritative view of current thinking. They are designed to provide easy-to-read and (most importantly) practical coverage of topics that are of interest to librarians and other information professionals. If you would like a full listing of current and forthcoming titles, please visit our web site **www.library-chandospublishing.com** or contact Hannah Grace-Williams on email info@chandospublishing.com or telephone number +44 (0) 1865 884447.

New authors: we are always pleased to receive ideas for new titles; if you would like to write a book for Chandos, please contact Dr Glyn Jones on email gjones@chandospublishing.com or telephone number +44 (0) 1865 884447.

Bulk orders: some organisations buy a number of copies of our books. If you are interested in doing this, we would be pleased to discuss a discount. Please contact Hannah Grace-Williams on email info@chandospublishing.com or telephone number +44 (0) 1865 884447.

The Role of the Legal Information Officer

TREVOR HARVEY

Chandos Publishing

Oxford · England

Chandos Publishing (Oxford) Limited
Chandos House
5 & 6 Steadys Lane
Stanton Harcourt
Oxford OX29 5RL
UK

Tel: +44 (0) 1865 884447 Fax: +44 (0) 1865 884448
Email: info@chandospublishing.com
www.library-chandospublishing.com

Chandos Publishing USA
3 Front Street, Suite 331
PO Box 338
Rollinsford, NH 03869
USA
Tel: 603 749 9171 Fax: 603 749 6155
Email: BizBks@aol.com

First published in Great Britain in 2003

ISBN:
1 84334 047 X (paperback)
1 84334 048 8 (hardback)

© T. Harvey, 2003

British Library Cataloguing-in-Publication Data.
A catalogue record for this book is available from the British Library.

Typeset by Monolith – www.monolith.uk.com
Printed in the UK and USA

Contents

Introduction

Of all the professions, information management is probably the one about which the man in the street has the most misconceptions. Tell the casual enquirer what you do for a living and you usually get the stock response of 'Isn't that rather boring?', but go into some detail of what your typical day as an information professional consists of and the response is quite different, something like: 'That sounds interesting!'

I have attempted in this book to give a flavour of what it is actually like to be a legal information professional in a City of London law firm at the beginning of the twenty-first century.

Many books on information management concentrate on the technical aspects of the profession. This book focuses on the practical aspects of what I believe is, first and foremost, a 'people' profession. Therefore, there is more about recruiting staff, promoting the information service and ways of getting know-how out of lawyers, and rather less on such matters as classification and indexing.

I have not only drawn on my experience as a legal information officer, but also from information posts I have held in the property information sector. While some of the practices and procedures described in the book refer specifically to the legal information sector, nearly all of them can be applied in any information environment.

I hope the book will be of interest to anybody who is thinking of becoming an information professional, whether they are at school or university or maybe at a later stage in their life when they are thinking of a career change. It will also be useful for any information professionals in the academic or public sectors either considering a move into the commercial environment or who wish to see what life is like 'on the other side'. Anyone considering a legal career (either from the perspective of a lawyer or an information professional) or who wants to know something about a support role in a global firm will also, I hope, find the book of interest.

I am fortunate in working for a firm which is very well resourced in terms of information systems, but I have endeavoured throughout the book to bear in mind that many legal information officers will not have the benefit of such a wide range of resources directly to hand.

I have also attempted to look into my crystal ball and tried to predict the future for the legal information professional over the next five to ten years. Many of my peers will not agree with my conclusions, but I have reached them based on my own experiences and observations of what is actually happening in the legal information environment.

A word about terminology. For many years now, the word 'librarian' has almost become extinct in the information world with most people in the profession preferring to identify themselves as information 'officers', 'managers' or 'professionals'. I have, in the main, used the term 'information officer' as this particular nomenclature is prevalent in the legal world but have also, on occasion, used the other descriptors in order to make a point or draw a comparison.

I must acknowledge two groups of people who have, in their different ways, contributed to this book. The first are my information colleagues, both in my present as well as my previous posts, who have, in many cases probably unknowingly, helped form my current views and opinions on information management. The second are the lawyers of the Financial Institutions Group, Clifford Chance London, who daily prove that the role of the legal information officer can be both enjoyable and stimulating.

The use of the masculine pronoun throughout the book includes by implication the female. Any errors and omissions are my own.

Trevor Harvey
Highbury, London
May 2003

About the author

Trevor Harvey was born in Sussex, attended schools in Brighton and Hove, and went to university in Wales where he gained a BA (Hons) in English and Classical Studies at University College, Cardiff. He later obtained a DipLib at the Polytechnic of North London. He has over twenty years' experience in information management and has held posts at the Royal Institution of Chartered Surveyors (RICS) and St Quintin, property consultants.

He joined global law firm Clifford Chance in 1997 where he set up their central information intranet. For the last three years he has been the Information Officer for the firm's Financial Insitutions Group, a group of sixty lawyers specialising in funds and insurance regulation. His professional interests include using the Internet for research and EU information. He is a regular contributor to the *FreePint* newsletter and a member of CILIP and the City Information Group.

The author can be contacted via the publishers.

Information roles and information sources

Qualifications

Information management, or librarianship as it was more commonly known about twenty years ago, is a graduate career and most people enter the profession either by gaining a first degree in any subject followed by a higher degree or postgraduate diploma in information studies or by gaining a first degree in information studies. In London and the larger legal provincial firms you may well find information personnel who have no information qualifications of any kind but who yet are involved in legal information work. Most will have law degrees and an increasing number are qualified lawyers.

Where are legal information professionals employed?

The British and Irish Association of Law Librarians (BIALL) website (*http://www.biall.org.uk/WEL11_where.asp*) provides a very useful checklist of the kinds of organisations where legal information professionals work. They include academic institutions, professional libraries such as the Law Society Library, the larger law firms and industry as well as national and local government.

Skills and aptitudes

Anyone who aspires to be an information professional needs to have or to develop the following skills and aptitudes:

A well-developed service ethos

Some readers may be surprised to see that I have put 'service ethos' at the top of the list. The bottom line is that the information profession is a service profession and if you are not prepared to put yourself out on behalf of others, then information work is not for you. This does not mean to say you have to be a 'doormat'. What it does mean is that you must be helpful with a willingness to be interested in other people's views and opinions.

Many people in the UK scoff at the American concept of service with such cheery mantras as 'Have a nice day now' and 'Your custom is important to us'. I am not advocating such extreme examples of solicitude but a lot can be learnt from the Americans' emphasis on providing good service. The art of providing a good information service is to put yourself in the enquirer's shoes and ask: 'Am I providing the level of service I would expect if I was on the other side of the enquiry desk?' If you have ever received unsatisfactory service from an establishment, whether it be a shop, pub, restaurant, hotel or library, the chances are you do not go back there again. Library users vote with their feet too.

An enquiring mind

You must enjoy undertaking research and thinking round a problem or 'thinking outside the box'. You must relish tracking down information and have the ability to assess and evaluate different types of information sources.

Good at dealing with pressure

The legal environment can be a very pressurised one, especially if a deal closure is imminent, and an ability to deal with pressure and not let things 'get on top of you' are essential attributes.

Well organised and methodical

You will need an ability to organise material, an aptitude for classification and cataloguing, and for constructing indexes, thesauri and databases. You will also need an ability to think on your feet and, as many legal information officers are solo operators or 'one-man bands', you must be able to organise yourself and to balance conflicting demands and roles.

Technical ability

In an increasingly electronic information environment, an understanding of how computers work and a familiarity with computer language and terminology is essential. The ability to empathise with IT staff and understand their role is also important.

Confident outgoing personality

You will be called upon to deal with a wide range of personality types in your information career so there is no room for that old cliché, the 'shy retiring librarian'. Apart from dealing with everyday users – and some lawyers can be very difficult, demanding people – you may be called upon to attend meetings (perhaps with a managing partner to present a case for an increase in your budget) or with suppliers to negotiate an agreement regarding a database you wish to purchase. You may have to give presentations and training sessions, whether it be in a one-to-one situation or addressing a large number of people in a meeting room or lecture theatre. The legal information world is no place for wallflowers or people who want to meld in with the background.

The various legal information roles

In this section I am going to examine the various information roles that can be found in a law firm. I have defined these roles by the *type* of work undertaken rather than by a job title because whether you are an 'information officer' or 'information researcher' you are essentially doing the same kind of work. In a larger firm different people will be assigned to different roles, but in a smaller firm one person may take on a number of roles.

Manager, director

This post entails:

- a senior role supervising staff and controlling a budget;
- a role as policy and decision-maker.

A managerial post can be a challenging and satisfying role in the sense that you have the potential to motivate your staff and develop your own ideas as to how your department should be run. The downside is the probability that you do not actually do any specific information work such as enquiries or indexing. You will inevitably come up against internal workplace politics which can defeat even the toughest operator.

One-man band, sole operator

In many firms, there is just one person responsible for information services with perhaps some part-time administrative assistance. You will be called upon to carry out the whole range of information work from the glamourous jobs such as research to the more mundane tasks like updating loose-leaf publications. If you have ambitions and big ideas, then the one-man-band scenario is probably not for you, but if you enjoy running your own show then being a 'sole operator' can be very enjoyable and stimulating.

I discuss further the role of the solo legal information professional in Chapter 9.

Research, dealing with enquiries

This is a front-line activity. The quality of your entire information service is often the benchmark by which user satisfaction is measured so it has got to be good. Enquiries can range from the quick reference type to those requiring more in-depth research.

Purchasing materials

I use the word 'materials' because in a twenty-first century information service it is not only books and journals that form part of your 'stock' but also and, perhaps to a greater extent, electronic databases. You will therefore have to liaise with publishers and database suppliers. If you intend to network your database across a firmwide intranet then you must take into account licensing and copyright considerations. You will be called upon to negotiate with database suppliers and copyright lawyers.

Cataloguing, classification, indexing, creating thesauri and taxonomies

Cataloguing and classification (cat 'n' class) was a staple part of any academic course in librarianship twenty years ago and, although currently such terms as 'thesaurus' and 'taxonomy' are more commonly used, the concept is essentially the same. You may be classifying material according to a prearranged scheme or you may be creating a system from scratch (either in paper format or electronically), particularly if you are working in a specialised area of law. This is an important 'behind-the-scenes' skill as the quality of your classification scheme determines how easily material can be accessed and located.

Inputting data, building and developing intranets

Increasingly, much of the information in law firms is disseminated over a firmwide intranet and developing and maintaining these intranets is a new role for information professionals that has become more prominent over the past few years. A good sense of design and screen layout is important.

Writing summaries and abstracts

Whether you are summarising material for an internal 'know-how' database or preparing a current awareness bulletin of news items, you will need to be able to identify the major points in a document and write a concise, meaningful summary of its contents.

Training and guidance

Whether helping lawyers with researching caselaw, locating relevant pages on the firm's intranet or finding useful information on the Internet, assisting users is an important part of the information professional's role. The training may be on an informal one-to-one basis at a fee earner's desk or presenting to a group in a formal meeting situation.

Administration

Under this heading I include those tasks which, while not particularly enjoyable, are essential to the smooth running of any information service, such as shelf tidying and updating loose-leaf encyclopaedias. There are also other 'behind-the-scenes' tasks such as record-keeping and filing of correspondence.

Stock

In this section I am going to look at the various materials that go to make up a typical law library or legal information department.

Hard copy

Books

Under this heading I include statutes, statutory instruments (SIs) and caselaw as well as legal textbooks and commentaries. Legal texts have always been an essential part of any law library of whatever size or description and, notwithstanding the development of electronic versions, always will be.

Cost and space will determine how many books you keep on your library shelves. Law texts can be expensive and you will have a budget to adhere to. You may also be limited by the amount of shelf space available. Another consideration will be the question of buying multiple copies of the most popular titles. Should each lawyer have his own personal copy? Should there be one copy per room (assuming, as is the case in most firms, that two or three lawyers share an office)? Should the library keep, say, four or five copies to meet everyday demand? The fact that some titles are now available in electronic format could impact on your purchasing decisions. How does the cost of purchasing the electronic version compare with the cost of purchasing multiple copies of the hard-copy version?

Some lawyers may be the firm's sole specialist in a particular area of the law and prefer to keep a collection of related textbooks in their office. This is a common practice in law firms. If the money to pay for these texts has come out of the 'library' budget, then you are quite justified in saying that even though they might be shelved in the lawyer's office, they can be consulted by *any* lawyer within the firm should the need arise.

It is not always advisable to dispose of an old edition of a textbook when the new one arrives. Sometimes a lawyer will need to consult the wording of a statute as it was at a certain date or check a statutory instrument that has subsequently been revoked. As textbooks (and any associated electronic versions) print the current version of the law, the appropriately dated earlier edition of the book could be the only possible source of the text.

Criteria for purchasing books

There is no mystique about the criteria you should adopt when deciding what books (or journals) to purchase for your library. It really is all down to common sense and if you do need advice on a particular book's merits or whether it covers its subject matter adequately, you can always ask one of the lawyers with whom you work. Many books will be purchased on the strength of a publisher's flyer or publicity, though if you have built up a good relationship with your supplier you may be able to view books 'on approval' with the option of returning them if you decide not to purchase. The following are just some of the questions you need to consider when deciding whether to purchase a book.

- Is the author a leading authority in his field?
- Is the book competitively priced in comparison with others of its type?
- Does it fill a gap in your collection?
- Does it approach its subject matter from a different viewpoint to other books on the same subject?
- Has it been recommended by a lawyer?
- Do other firm's law libraries have copies?
- Will it be used by your lawyers in their day-to-day work?
- How many of your lawyers will consult it regularly?

Loose-leaf encyclopaedias

Loose-leaf encyclopaedias are another staple ingredient of the law library in which hole-punched pages are filed in (usually) A5 folders thus enabling pages to be easily removed and replaced by later versions. This type of publication is obviously going to be more current and up to date than any book, but it is important that the new pages are filed as soon as they arrive on your desk because without these updates the loose-leaf is useless.

I have often noticed a certain reluctance on the part of information staff to regularly update loose-leaf encyclopaedias and a backlog is allowed to build up. Apart from rendering the publication out of date, filing updates is a very good way of keeping abreast of developments in the law.

It should hardly need to be stressed that it is the responsibility of the information officer who purchases publications to ensure that the copy of the text on the library shelves is the current edition and that all the loose-leaf updates have been filed. Lawyers are relying on these texts when they are giving advice to clients and they need to be assured they are using an up-to-date copy. One of the most frequent questions I am asked by lawyers who use loose-leaf encyclopaedias is 'When was it last updated?' It is helpful to create a page at the front of the loose-leaf (if the publisher has not already done so) where you can indicate the dates on which it has been updated.

Journals

In the pre-electronic era, journals (also known as magazines or periodicals and, to a lesser extent, serials) assumed a great importance as the one information tool that reflected current thought and opinion on a particular subject, mainly due to their regular publication schedule. This pre-eminent position as the most topical and current source of information to be found in any library (with the possible exception of newspapers) has been dented in recent years by the advent of electronic news services. Increasingly, too, a journal will also be produced in an electronic version, either in full text or just offering selected articles as a 'taster' with the rest of the contents available after a subscription has been taken out.

Journals generally come in two types. The first is the 'academic', usually published at monthly or quarterly intervals containing lengthy analytical articles. The second type adopts a more 'newsy' format consisting of shorter articles and is usually published at weekly intervals. The big plus point for journals is their flexibility; they can be taken into meetings, read on train or air journeys, and articles can be photocopied and disseminated to interested parties (subject to copyright considerations). They are excellent for browsing and serendipity, that is coming across an article which is on a subject of interest to you but is not one you had been actively seeking out.

A widespread practice in many law firms is to circulate a copy of the entire journal among interested members of staff. A slip is attached to the front cover of each title listing the names of all those who wish to read it. Once the first person on the list has read the journal, he then passes it on to the next person on the list and so on until everyone has seen it and the journal is then shelved in the library. The major benefit of this system is that the browsing/serendipity factor mentioned above comes into play; the major disbenefit is the time it can take for the journal to circulate to everyone who wants to see it.

With a large circulation list, this can cause major problems and those unfortunate people at the bottom of the list sometimes only get to see a journal long after it has lost its currency and topicality. This does not matter so much with journals published at quarterly intervals, but for those which appear monthly, and particularly weekly, the situation is far from satisfactory. It can be alleviated by purchasing multiple copies of journals and dividing up a long circulation list between the copies or subscribing to the electronic version. But there's no getting away from the fact that people do 'sit on journals' and are reluctant to send them on within, say, 24 hours. The situation is further exacerbated when someone is away from the office sick or on holiday and unread journals pile up on his desk.

If some kind of current awareness news service is provided (whether in-house or purhcased from an external source) I have found that this has the effect of reducing the demand for the widespread circulation of journals as the news service distills all the information that would otherwise have been gleaned from the perusal of the hard-copy journal and the frequency of the current awareness service ensures that currency is achieved.

Shelving journals

The best way of shelving journals is to store them in specially designed upright magazine files, made either of cardboard or plastic, which can be purchased from major high-street stationery stores or specialist library suppliers.

A major policy decision for any information officer is how far back copies of a particular journal title should be kept. For each journal, the following points will need to be considered:

- How much shelf space is available?

- How important is the journal and its contents to the firm's business? Is it frequently consulted? How big is its circulation list? How often are copies of its articles requested?

- Do its contents date quickly? Does it cover an area of law that changes a lot or one which is fairly static?

- How easy is it to obtain back numbers or photocopies of articles, either from the publisher of the journal or from an organisation that supplies photocopied journal articles,[1] and what is the cost of doing so?

- Is it available in an electronic format?

- Does any other person or department within the firm (or even a neighbouring law firm) keep back copies and how quick and/or easy would it be to obtain them?

Once a decision has been made for each title it is a simple matter of making a note on the front of the magazine holder showing the length of the journal run (e.g. 'two years', 'three years', 'six months') which will assist users when they are browsing.

An effective way of weeding out journals is to use what I call the 'weed as you go' method. When filing the latest copy of a journal in its magazine holder, remove the very first copy from the holder, thus saving the need for a mammoth weeding out session once or twice a year.

Know-how

'Know-how' is documentation generated within the firm as a result of a deal or project undertaken by its lawyers. Know-how is further discussed in Chapter 7.

Electronic

Databases, CD-Rom, Internet, intranet

A number of legal sources are now available free of charge on the Internet and anyone can access them at any time, but other electronic sources, such as commercially available databases consisting of news items and journal articles in full text, have to be paid for and a decision has to be taken as to how widely available these should be made throughout the firm and to whom. The following points should be considered when making such a decision (I use the word 'system' to cover any electronic source of information, whether it be a database or CD-Rom):

- How user friendly is the system?
- Would users need to receive training in how to use it?
- Is there the staff and resources to run an effective training programme?
- Will the suppliers of the system permit multiple access?
- What are the licensing agreements?
- Will individual passwords have to be set up?
- Will the number of users permitted to use the system at any one time be restricted?

It makes sense, in many cases, for those databases that have a strong legal content to be made available to all lawyers via their PCs. However, costs may dictate that such extensive access is not possible and this will impact on information staff time and resources as it is inevitable that many more database search requests will be filtered through to the information department. The database may only be made available on a walk-up PC in the library area and users will require assistance in using it from trained information staff.

The level of access by the end user will also depend on the policy adopted by the firm: whether total end user access is encouraged or a more restrictive approach adopted whereby only information staff carry out searches. The type of law firm will also impact on this decision: lawyers in a global 24-hour law firm dealing with a range of clients across the world working in different time zones will need to have access to the databases at any time and as 24-hour information services in the big law firms are not yet the norm (though some of the big investment banks do have them) the lawyers will be undertaking many of their own searches. A smaller niche firm whose range of work and clients is narrower may prefer the information staff to undertake database searches.

The final decision about the level of access allowed to lawyers will come down to the question of cost. It is unwise to let lawyers loose on a database where access is charged on a 'pay as you go basis' as costs would soar. If you intend to make a database widely available to lawyers, then it would be more cost-effective to negotiate a deal whereby you pay a lump sum upfront for unlimited usage.

Hard copy vs electronic version

Many law textbooks, journals and loose-leaf encyclopaedias are available nowadays in both hard copy and electronic versions. Whether you purchase one or the other type or opt for a mixture of the two will be dictated by a number of factors; both versions have their advantages and disadvantages.

The first consideration is the level of the firm's technological development – obviously, if a firm's lawyers do not have their own desktop PCs then the library is going to be very much book based. But assuming that everyone does have their own desktop PC, is the Internet generally available? This is an important consideration as many electronic sources of information nowadays utilise Internet technology as a means of transmission. Many publications are available on CD. Can these be networked across the firm?

Remember also that law is a document-rich profession. It is only in the last five years that electronic versions of standard texts have really come to the fore; historically, the law was only available in bound volumes and there may be a resistance, particularly on the part of older lawyers, to the electronic revolution.

The way lawyers work must also be taken into account: documents need to be drafted and redrafted, different parts of a statute, or different statutes, may need to be compared, a word or phrase defined from another source – tasks that are easier to undertake by having a number of sources in hard copy spread out on a desk or table for comparison rather than trying to access their electronic equivalents on a computer. Health and safety considerations (the advice is to look away from the screen every 15 minutes) preclude the reading of lengthy chunks of text on screen and studies have shown that people 'read' computer screens differently from the way they read books, in that they 'scan' or 'skim' text on screen. The reality is that a lot of documentation will be downloaded and printed from databases.

A total reliance on electronic versions leaves you high and dry if the computer crashes. On the other hand, books 'walk' and go missing from the shelves. Rows and rows of books can occupy costly floorspace; computers can hold vast libraries of data. The electronic version of a text is always going to be more current than the book which cannot be updated until another edition is published. If a book's electronic version is transmitted over the Internet for example, it could be updated daily; even a CD may be updated monthly. A legal text is out of date the moment it is published, especially if it covers an area of law which is constantly changing.

However, having English law as an electronic source does have a distinct advantage over the hard copy. In pre-electronic days, if you wanted to ensure that a piece of English legislation was up to date, you had to go through a process of consulting maybe up to two further publications. Similarly, if you wanted to check whether a piece of secondary legislation had been produced which related to the statute you were looking at, you had to consult another two different sources. With the electronic version, you have the consolidated up-to-date text with access to any related secondary legislation at the click of a mouse button. The research time has been reduced dramatically.

The electronic version has so much more flexibility too. If a statute makes reference to another piece of legislation, you can link directly to the appropriate document. You can (subject to copyright considerations) cut and paste text and send it on (again, subject to copyright considerations) to a third party.

Electronic versions do tend to be more expensive than the hard copy, though you may be able to negotiate a deal with the system's suppliers whereby you can have both. It is easier to take books into a client meeting rather than set up the technology to enable you to access the data on screen (particularly if the meeting is called at short notice). On the other hand, if a lawyer is giving a lecture or presentation to clients then being able to access texts available over the firm's intranet during the course of his talk will add considerably to the presentation's value and impact.

In the end, the choice of whether you purchase a book's hard copy or electronic version will come down to a combination of cost and working practices. A total reliance on electronic sources is just not suitable for the way lawyers work and most firms will opt for a mixture of the two formats which should meet all eventualities. For example, a standard text on company law will be purchased as well as its electronic version; one (the hard copy) is a working document, the other (the electronic) is a research tool.

Note

1. Such as DocDel (*http://www.smlawpub.co.uk/products/docdel/docdel.cfm*) or the British Library.

2

Managing and recruiting

Managing

In this section I am going to look at the role of the manager from the point of view of someone who manages a number of staff so the emphasis will be on personnel issues rather than the management of information or of oneself.

In over twenty years in the information profession, the first thing that strikes me about managers who manage a team of information professionals is how removed they are from core library and information work. Not one of the bosses I have reported to ever did enquiry work – in fact the one occasion a boss of mine did sit on the enquiry desk due to a severe staff shortage he quickly revealed his lack of skills as a 'reference/enquiry librarian'. However, many information professionals are attracted to a senior managerial position where they can implement ideas and strategies, direct policies and run matters as they would wish.

During my years in the information profession I have worked for a number of managers and have experienced a number of different management styles. Based on my observations I have drawn up a list of procedures which represent managerial best practice. A good manager will set the tone and style of his department and this can be achieved in a number of ways. Anyone adopting all of these ideas would, I submit, prove to be an exceptional information manager.

- If you have meetings with senior partners at which strategies and future developments concerning the firm and its library and information service are discussed, report back (taking into account any questions of confidentiality), keeping your staff in the picture.

- Have regular team meetings (at least once a week) with all your staff. Make these formal (i.e. have an agenda where anyone can raise matters) but also encourage an informal atmosphere so that no one is inhibited from making a contribution.

- Encourage your staff to come up with new ideas and ways of doing things.

- Encourage attendance at courses and seminars.

- Continually look at ways of developing your staff – do not just give new projects to those you know will do them well. Give a push to those members of your staff who need a push. Ensure that your staff fulfil their potential.

- Deal with any problems as they occur – do not allow matters to fester. If you are unhappy with one of your staff's performance or attitude, raise it as soon as possible; do not leave it until the annual appraisal when the particular circumstances may have changed and the moment has passed.

- Always make your criticisms constructive criticisms and never ever criticise a member of staff in front of his colleagues.

- Be ready to praise a member of staff if they have performed particularly well on a certain occasion.

- Carry out annual staff appraisals.

- Seek guidance from the personnel department regarding disciplinary matters (e.g. persistent lateness, poor attendance record).

- Always be approachable so that any member of your staff would feel no qualms in raising any concerns they may have with you.

- On the other hand, maintain a certain distance from your staff in order to ease the resolution of any discipline problems. It is difficult to get the balance just right on this one, but I have observed situations where a manager wishing to be seen as just another one of the boys or girls has lost the respect of his staff because of his behaviour.

- Create a procedures manual so that there is a standard uniform way of doing everything from how the telephone should be answered to the criteria for assessing the purchase of an online database. (Procedures manuals seem to be rare beasts in the library and information world: of the seven posts I have held in the last twenty years, only one library had a procedures manual and yet I see it as an essential management tool, particularly if you employ temporary or contract staff.)

- Always look at new ways of doing things. Just because a particular procedure has always been followed, do not assume that it is the best way. On the other hand, 'if it ain't broke, don't fix it' – in other words, do not change things for the sake of change.

- Be bold – have big ideas and carry them through. Listen to people's objections, but if you feel it is the right way to proceed, go ahead and do it explaining why you think it should be done.
- Admit your mistakes.
- Do not stand over your staff watching their every move but ensure that you are aware of what they are doing so that you can make constructive comments at their annual appraisal.

And so, you have the perfect manager! In reality, of course, the manager will come up against a number of stumbling blocks to achieving his desires: office politics, lack of commitment from the partnership, budgetary constraints and the attitude of the staff he employs.

However many ideas he has for developing and improving the library and information service, unless the manager is supported by the firm's managing partners he is going to find his role a frustrating one. This means not just financial support in terms of setting a budget but moral support in terms of supporting his ideas and aims. What often happens in the larger firms is that a partner in one particular practice area will be very supportive of what his information manager does while another from a different practice area will provide no support at all.

Recruiting

At some point in your career as an information officer, even if you will be working mainly on your own as a solo professional, you will have to go through the process of recruiting staff, an area which is fraught with problems and pitfalls for the unwary.

This section consists of my observations on recruitment drawn from my own experience both as an interviewer and interviewee over the course of twenty years.

Finding staff

There are basically two main ways of recruiting information staff: the first is to place an advertisement in an appropriate source; the second is to register the vacancy with a recruitment agency. An advertisement can be placed in a journal or newspaper and, of course, nowadays will probably also appear in the publication's electronic version. Jobs also appear on the various information-related discussion lists. Placing an advertisement means that you retain more control over the whole recruitment process in that you can word the advertisement to suit your own specifications and select candidates for interview after sifting through the applications you receive. This can be a very time-consuming process even though you may have the assistance and support of your personnel department.

Placing a job with a specialist recruitment agency (or agencies) removes much of the tedious sifting through of applications and CVs (curricula vitae) leaving you free to concentrate on interviewing the candidates that the agency puts forward. You are, of course, giving away control over the whole selection process and relying on the judgement of others to select appropriate candidates for interview, and however well you have briefed the agency there is still room for mismatches. Recruitment agencies, in my experience, tend to 'pigeon hole' the candidates on their books and will focus on people who have the right background and experience for the post, thus excluding those who, while not possessing the 'correct fit', do have the necessary aptitude and desire to make a change.

Making your intentions clear at the outset

Whether you are placing an advertisement yourself or registering a vacancy with an agency you must be specific about the kind of candidates you are hoping to attract. Such specifications usually fall into two categories: the essential and the desirable. The essential might include a certain level of education to have been reached and relevant experience gained while desirable might include linguistic competency and knowledge of particular databases.

When recruiting legal information staff, one of the most important decisions you will have to make will be how essential it is that the person you eventually appoint should have some kind of legal background. The nature of the post may mean that a legal background is not necessary while in other cases it would be desirable. A good information professional should be able to transfer skills from one sector to another; proven success in one area of information work should not preclude success in another. I shall further discuss this dichotomy between legal and information qualified personnel in Chapter 10.

Reading a CV or application form

There is so much advice available nowadays on constructing a CV (and I deliberately use the word 'construct' rather than 'write') that it appears that every candidate is proactive, dynamic, enjoys a challenge and is an enthusiastic team player. The reality of the interview situation, and indeed the work environment, confirms that this is not so.

However, the CV plus covering letter (or application form) is all that you have to go on (initially) when selecting candidates for interview. A candidate is putting himself in the best possible light so that you are prompted to call him in for interview and discover whether he is suitable for the job. The art of reading a CV is trying to discover what has been left unsaid as much as what has been said.

If the CV (or covering letter) in front of you contains any of these features, alarm bells should start ringing:

- Watch out for any CV that is not typewritten or word processed. Beware of individualistic tendencies such as green ink or paper other than standard white.

- CVs should not be more than two or, if you are recruiting a more mature candidate, three pages long. Anything over this number of pages smacks of desperation with a tendency to embroider details of posts held and build them up to be more than they actually were.

- Watch out for gaps between jobs: make sure the information about the period between jobs has been explained on the CV and that gaps in an employment record do not conceal more sinister reasons.

- Beware of the candidate who changes jobs frequently and ask yourself why they have done so. Have they not fitted in? Did they lack commitment? You do have to be a little careful here, because many people nowadays have deliberately chosen contract and temporary work as a career path, but the astute candidate will have made this clear elsewhere on the CV.

- On the other hand, beware of the candidate who has stayed in the same job or organisation for a very long time (unless they have moved posts within that organisation). Do they lack drive and energy? Are they complacent? Lazy?

- Beware of the CV that has been prepared by a specialist firm on the candidate's behalf. You can usually spot these by the terminology employed (there will just be too much management jargon) and the CV itself will have a certain 'over-prepared' look about it. There is nothing inherently wrong in a candidate getting someone else to construct their CV for them, but it does give the impression that they cannot think for themselves.

- Do not forget to look at the hobbies and interests section. Some of those experts who specialise in preparing CVs are now advising candidates that it is no longer necessary to make reference to leisure pursuits on a CV but I disagree, as this gives the impression that the candidate is a sad individual who has no life outside work (however true that may be).

It should hardly need saying that at no stage in the interview process should you discriminate against any candidate on the grounds of race, sex, age, religious belief, sexual orientation or political affiliation.

The covering letter gives the candidate the opportunity to really sell himself and allow his character and personality to come over. This is particularly important if, on the basis of his CV alone, the candidate does not appear to be suitable for the post. This is his chance to convince you that he is.

One of the most interesting parts of a CV is the reasons given for leaving a particular job as this is the one area where a certain massaging of the truth really does come into play. So we get reasons such as 'promotion', 'broadening of experience' and the one I particularly like, 'furthering my career', when in reality I have found that most people leave a job for one of two reasons: 'more money' or they 'did not get on with their boss'.

The next stage in the recruitment process, the interview, is where you discover whether the candidate matches the promises shown on their CV.

The interview

It may be that you have gone through a number of years in the information profession without actually having to interview anyone, and while having been an interviewee yourself will have provided you with a number of tips and pointers about how to conduct (as well as how not to conduct) an interview, it is the case that the interview process can be as nerve racking for the interviewer as it is for the interviewee.

As a good information professional you will have read some articles or a book on interviewing, but it would also be advisable to speak to your personnel department and ask for their guidance. A member of the personnel team should also ideally be part of the interviewing panel as their expertise and input is important in helping you make the right decision about who should be made a job offer.

Even if it is just a preliminary interview it is always best anyway to have at least one other person assisting you even if only as an observer. A second opinion on a candidate's potential is always worthwhile and the other person will often pick up on comments made by the candidate that you may have missed.

A good interview should be seen almost as a conversation; you should, in no way, approach it in order to score points off a candidate or make them feel uncomfortable. The purpose of an interview is to ensure that you employ the best available candidate for the job. You should be as well prepared as you hope the candidates themselves will be; always go into an interview with a prepared set of questions and make notes as it progresses to aid the post-interview discussion.

The style and course of an interview will depend on the vacancy in question and the maturity of the interviewees. An interview for a job designed for a school or college leaver will be different from one for a senior management post. In all instances, though, you are looking for someone who will fit in with the culture and ethos of the firm or department, who has the right attitude and who will get on with his colleagues. Not too much to ask really.

As with CVs, there are a few things you need to be on your guard about when conducting interviews:

- Make sure your questions are of the open ended type, i.e. that they are designed to elicit more than a 'yes' or 'no' response. In other words, do not ask 'Do you pay attention to detail?' but rather ask 'Can you give me some examples of how you pay attention to detail?'

- Do not stick rigidly to a set of prepared questions. A candidate will often make a comment that needs following up so be prepared to go down routes you had not planned.

- Be alert to body language. For example, be wary of the candidate who brings their hand up to their mouth when answering a question – they may not be giving a completely truthful answer.

- Even if you have decided within the first five minutes that the candidate is not suitable, you must plough on and complete the interview. Conversely, some candidates take time to blossom so do not always write people off in the first five minutes.

- Try to differentiate between the confident and the arrogant candidate. The latter will make boasts and claims that the skilful interviewer will be able to repudiate.

- Do not be taken in by candidates who have been groomed especially for the interview or whose answers seem 'over-prepared'. A follow-up question to an assertion they have made will generally expose the weakness of their original statement. Also, be on the lookout for the repetition of certain words or phrases in contexts in which they do not seem appropriate. This is another sign of the weaker candidate having been groomed.

- Look beyond the jargon. If a candidate says that they are a good team player, ask them to give you an example of that particular quality.

- If you are anxious to ensure that your new member of staff has the 'right attitude' and will fit in with the rest of your hand-picked team, ask questions such as 'Why do you think librarians and information professionals have such a bad image?' or 'How do you deal with disappointments and setbacks?'

- Go with your instincts. If you feel a candidate is being economical with the truth about a certain matter, such as the reason why they left a particular job or the length of time they were with a certain company, press them until you get a satisfactory response.

- If you want to ascertain a candidate's commitment to an information career ask them about their intentions of becoming a member of CILIP or pursuing chartership with the same organisation. Due to the competition for training contracts, many law graduates turn to legal information work as a stopgap while they look for a vacancy as a trainee solicitor, so you may want to try and discover their true intentions. There is nothing wrong in a 'wannabe' lawyer applying for an information post, but do not be surprised if six months down the line they resign because they have found a training contract in a firm, leaving you in the position of having to start the recruitment process all over again.

However skilful you are as an interviewer, how careful you have been with your initial sorting of CVs and application forms, however many discussions you have had with your interviewer colleagues over the suitability of the candidates on offer, there is still an element of luck involved in recruitment and selecting the candidate to whom you make a job offer. The savvy candidate is well prepared and will say in the interview what he knows you *want* to hear him say, and so while he has assured you of his credentials of being an effective team player, once in post he may well reveal himself as a maverick and a loner.

Once the offer has been made to your preferred candidate, you must be prepared for the fact that he could turn you down. Good candidates may have other job offers in the pipeline or have decided that your particular vacancy is not what they were looking for. It is always advisable to have a second or third candidate lined up just in case this eventuality should occur.

References

'Not worth the paper they are written on', a former boss of mine once said about references, and there is a lot of truth in that throwaway remark. Due in part to concerns about being sued by former employees, many employers simply state in a reference the dates of the candidate's employment and details of their absence and attendance records. For similar reasons, former employers are also reluctant to provide telephone references as these are as legally binding as written ones. Except in particular circumstances, there is no legal requirement anyway for an employer to provide a reference for current or past employees.

Keeping staff happy

Once your new member of staff has joined the firm, you must ensure that they remain happy contented workers and find the work satisfying and fulfilling.

One of the first things to be considered after your new recruit has started work is the type of training you are going to offer him. One method is to assign the new appointee another member of your staff as a mentor or guide for the first few days or weeks to 'show them the ropes'. For this set-up to work effectively, much depends on the qualities of the person that has been assigned and their teaching abilities. The assigner may resent being taken away from their normal work and this attitude could come across to the new staff member thus giving him a very bad first impression of the firm he has joined.

If you have a large number of staff it would be better for each staff member who has responsibilities in certain areas (e.g. book purchasing, journals control, cataloguing) to have short sessions with the new recruit in order to explain their particular area of expertise. In this way, the training load is spread among all the team, even those who might profess a certain reluctance to carry out this role. Do not forget that the training process can be as much of a benefit to the trainer as the trainee as they are learning the skills of putting ideas across to another person thus improving their own communication skills at the same time.

Where a firm only has only two or three information staff, the opportunities for on-the-job training may be limited and new members of staff will be left more to find their own way.

Do not expect your new member of staff to hit the ground running. Some people take time to bed into a job and the right attitude and approach to the work is more important than how quickly they assimilate the subject knowledge and learn new skills.

Most firms have a probationary period, usually three months, after which the appointment is confirmed. You may be generally happy with the new member of staff's performance, but if there are any areas of concern, these should be raised now at the end of this three-month period.

If there are serious shortcomings at any time with the performance of any of your staff which may involve verbal or written warnings, then you must involve someone from your personnel department in order to ensure that internal guidelines and the relevant law are being adhered to. If serious disciplinary issues do arise with any of your staff, it is prudent to involve the personnel department as soon as possible.

It is all too easy to ignore performance-related problems and hope they will go away, but if there are serious shortcomings they need to be addressed. Do not wait for the annual appraisal before raising any concerns you may have.

Readers may think I have focused too much on the negative aspects of CVs and interviews, but I really think it is important to be cautious and sceptical in the light of certain statements on CVs and responses at interview. The consequences of appointing the wrong candidate can be wide-ranging for the firm, the rest of the information department and, not least, the candidate himself.

3

Marketing and promoting your service

Any information service, even one that is successful and well used with a high level of user satisfaction, can benefit from marketing itself. This not only serves to remind users of services offered by the information department of which they may previously have been unaware, but it is an opportunity for the information officer to be innovative and come up with ideas on how to develop and improve the service he offers. In the process, both the profiles of his department and of himself are raised.

Some marketing ideas we will consider in this chapter are:

- current awareness;
- team meetings;
- training:
  - library tours;
  - presentations and seminars;
  - one-to-one training.

Current awareness

One of the most effective ways of promoting the information service in a law firm is to have some kind of current awareness service in place so that laywers can keep up to date with developments in their particular field.

However, before reading this section on current awareness, I would recommend that you read Chapter 8 on copyright. It hardly needs to be stressed that a legal information officer should be particularly alert to the infringement of copyright. So, with a rider to the effect that most, if not all, of the following current awareness products will involve a consideration of copyright issues, please read on.

Photocopying contents pages

The most basic form of current awareness is photocopying the contents pages of journals, circulating them to staff who then request copies of any of the articles that interest them. In these days of 'e-mail alerts', photocopying contents pages is rather an old-fashioned form of current awareness and probably works best in a small niche practice where other types of awareness, either for reasons of cost or staff time, are not suitable. However, the photocopying of the requested articles can be a time-consuming activity in itself. There is the additional consideration that the mere title of an article as printed on a contents page is not always a helpful indicator as to its actual content.

Doing it yourself

I have always found producing current awareness bulletins to be one of the most satisfying aspects of information work. From a purely self-interested point of view, it is an excellent way of keeping up to speed with what is happening in your particular area of law. They are always well received by lawyers who appreciate being kept up to date in this way. Reading a one- or two-page current awareness bulletin removes the need for the busy practitioner to read a number of journals and may also help reduce the problem of journals sitting in lawyers' in-trays and not being passed on to the next reader quickly.

The first thing to consider is whether it is actually worthwhile producing a current awareness bulletin in-house or purchasing one that is already produced by someone else. There may be something on the market which will suit your purposes admirably and you will need to weigh up the cost of purchasing it compared to the staff costs and time involved in producing your own. If you are working in a very specialised area of the law, you may discover either that there is nothing on the market that covers your topic adequately or that the sources used in compiling the bulletin do not fit the particular slant of the legal practice in which you work. In addition, the cost of subscribing to a ready-made bulletin may be outside your budget.

Sources used for compiling a current awareness bulletin

The following sources could all be used in compiling a current awareness bulletin:

- newspaper and journal articles;
- government press releases;

- bills and debates on new legislation;

- forthcoming conferences and seminars;

- new book stock added to the library;

- know-how added to the database;

- recent caselaw;

- announcements from relevant professional associations and organisations.

Frequency of publication

You must think very carefully before committing yourself to the regular production of a current awareness bulletin. If you promise, for example, to produce a *daily* newsletter, it must be a daily newsletter; you cannot use the excuse of pressure of work to avoid publication on a busy day or when staff are absent. If you have raised expectations in your users, you must live up to them. A daily or weekly publication will obviously have more currency than one that appears monthly.

The publication schedule will determine the contents of the bulletin. It is no good including news items in a bulletin that will appear a month later as the item will be long past its 'sell by date'. If we look again at our checklist of sources we can categorise each one according to whether it would be more suitable for use in a weekly or a monthly current awareness bulletin:

- *Weekly*:
  - summaries of items from daily newspapers;
  - summaries of articles that appear in journals published weekly;

- government press releases;
- forthcoming conferences and seminars.

■ *Monthly*:
- new book stock added to the library;
- know-how added to the database;
- recent caselaw;
- summaries of articles that appear in journals published monthly.

The list is not prescriptive of course as items which appear under the 'Weekly' heading, like government press releases and forthcoming conferences and seminars, could very well be included in a monthly publication but would lose their topicality if they were (e.g. the conference booking period may well have closed).

Writing abstracts

It is more than likely that the greater part of any current awareness bulletin will consist of summaries of items that have appeared in newspapers and journals. In order to convey the content and flavour of the original article, you will need to write a summary or 'abstract' of that article.

Basically, abstracts fall into two broad categories: the 'indicative' and the 'descriptive'.

Indicative

The indicative abstract merely gives a flavour of the article or highlights its main headings, as in the following example:

Title: Corporate taxation strategy in Guernsey

Date: 22 November 2002

Summary: Including banks, fiduciaries, insurance managers, fund managers, collective investment schemes, closed-ended funds, domestic insurers and offshore insurers.

Descriptive

A descriptive abstract will quote significant sections of the article which are its core points or arguments, as in the following example:

Title: Listing property funds on the Irish Stock Exchange

Date: January 2003

Summary: Key property fund requirements: there must be at least two directors who are independent of the investment manager and investment adviser, they must be passive investors but may take legal and management control of underlying properties. They must also comply with the general investment restrictions imposed by the ISE which include adhering to the general principle of risk spreading.

Tips on writing abstracts

The article

There is usually no need to read the whole article unless you want to or have the time to do so. The combined pressures of deadlines and other articles to précis usually dictates that a complete read-through is impossible and anyway, for the purposes of summarising, it should be sufficient to scan an article. Scanning means running your eyes over the text alighting on sentences and words that stand out as meaningful and important.

Look at the structure of the article and see if the way it has been laid out will assist you in getting an idea of what it is all about. Does the opening paragraph summarise all the main points of the entire article? (This is often the way newspaper articles are written – the major thrust or conclusion of the article is contained in the first paragraph which draws the reader in, making him want to read the rest of it.) Check out the final paragraph too – that may provide a handy summing up. Is the article divided up into headings and subheadings? Does one paragraph lead on logically to the next? In other words, use the layout of the article as a guide to getting an idea of the content of the whole piece.

A word of warning: although many articles already have a printed abstract at the head of the item, do not assume you can rely on it and reproduce it in your own bulletin. The abstract may be focusing on aspects of the article that do not entirely match with the particular interests of the readers of your own bulletin, so you need to prepare one that is relevant for them.

If the article in question is not well laid out with helpful subject paragraphs and headings, how do you go about focusing on those aspects of it that are important and which must be included in an abstract?

Look out for linguistic clues, such as:

'The most important points about this case are...'

'An interesting feature of this report is...'

'It is agreed by most practitioners that...'

'John Smith, one of the leading experts in his field, commented that...'

Any of the above phrases could be completed in such a way as to provide important or unusual information which could warrant inclusion in your abstract. As you become more adept at scanning articles, you will pick up on these linguistic clues more readily.

You will never be able to include all the major points of an article in an abstract so do not try to do so.

As you scan the article, write down what you think are its important facts or major findings. The type and style of the article may dictate whether you prepare an indicative or a descriptive abstract, or you may have decided that your bulletin will use one or other type or a mixture of both. Generally, I have found that short articles lend themselves more to being summarised by an indicative abstract and longer ones by a descriptive abstract, but this should not be taken as a hard and fast rule. As you look over the article's salient points that you have jotted down, the type of abstract may immediately present itself to you. One can be summarised in a couple of sentences; another will contain meatier ideas that must be included.

Problem articles: waffle and incomprehension

One of the hardest types of article to summarise is the one that says nothing at all but is full of 'waffle' and 'padding' and where the author could have expressed his ideas in two pages rather than the six he ended up with. Do not be tempted to criticise the content of an article – for one thing you are laying yourself open to the possibility of libel – but it is a good rule of thumb when writing abstracts to provide just a concise factual summary. An astute reader may be able to read 'between the lines' anyway and deduce any implied criticism. Look at the following abstract of a (fictional) article:

Title: The Financial Services and Markets Act 2000

Author: Smith, James

Journal: *Law for Everyone*, 1(3), June 2000, pp. 3–12

The author summarises in three pages the important features of this major piece of legislation.

This is a simplistic abstract but the point is that the canny reader will have noted that although the article's total number of pages comes to ten (pp. 3–12), the abstracter has written that 'the author summarises in *three* pages', the implication being that the rest of the article is unnecessary waffle. You must be very sure of yourself, your skills as an abstracter and your knowledge of the subject matter on which are you writing to produce a 'critical' abstract, however implied that criticism is.

The abstract

KISS

Keep your writing style simple and to the point following the KISS principle (Keep It Simple and Straightforward – a common acronym used in marketing). Use short sentences and avoid redundant words and phrases that add nothing to the meaning of the sentence. For example, do not write:

'This new statute completely revises the 1929 version'.

Just write:

'This new statute revises the 1929 version'.

Avoid over-punctuating your text and using parentheses as this gives a cluttered, fussy look. This should be particularly borne in mind if your abstracts will appear in electronic format on a computer screen.

Don't forget the title!

There is no need to repeat the title of the article, or information contained in the title, in the body of the abstract. Think of the title as an integral part of your abstract.

What do you really mean?

Avoid ambiguities. These often occur in newspaper headlines where journalists, keen to attract the reader with snappy headlines, will use a shorthand which is universally recognised but which might in other circumstances cause confusion. For example, a headline might read:

Halifax soars ahead

Increased prosperity for the town of Halifax in Yorkshire as a result of a new company moving in? No, increased profits for the Halifax Building Society actually. Even if you retain the 'Halifax' in the headline, you must ensure that you include the name 'Halifax Building Society' in the actual abstract itself to ensure clarity of meaning.

Don't be too colloquial

Many statutes and regulations are known by a popular name as a form of shorthand to avoid quoting the title in full. Your abstract may refer to the proposed 'Savings Directive' but you should also include its full title ('Proposal for a Council directive to ensure effective taxation of savings income in the form of interest payments within the Community') and any references (in this case COM 2001/0400) to assist the reader in locating quickly a copy of the full proposal should they wish to do so. If the correct title and reference details are not provided in the article itself, you must ensure that you obtain them yourself from a reliable source.

Another 'shorthand' problem area concerns the cavalier use of company names. If the author of the article you are summarising refers to a [fictional] company as 'Harvey & Jones' throughout the article, but as you scan the text, it turns out that he is actually referring to one of its subsidiaries 'Harvey & Jones (London) Ltd' then again you must make that point clear when writing the abstract.

Being precise about names and titles and tidying up lazy journalism is especially important if your abstracts will be searchable as a full-text database or index. In the example above, one user may search under 'Savings Directive', another may look for the European Commission reference COM 2001/0400. It is essential that both references are included in your abstract so that all searching eventualities are covered.

Method of delivery

Even in a firm where e-mail is the standard way of transmitting information, it may be worth considering producing your current awareness bulletin in hard-copy format. In these days when people are continuously bombarded with e-mails, producing something in hard copy has the effect of making that product stand out, simply because it has not been delivered electronically.

Information overload

The development of e-mail has added considerably to the problem of information overload. The amount of information popping up in lawyers' e-mail inboxes these days is overwhelming. In the City fim where I currently work, there are at least six commercially available e-mail alert services that lawyers can sign up to, not counting the various alerter services that newspapers and journals provide. There is a danger that your carefully wrought, well-crafted in-house bulletin will just get lost amid all the other current awareness products.

Ad hoc current awareness

You may decide that the time and effort spent in producing a current awareness bulletin is not worth the hassle and that what lawyers already receive from external sources suits their purposes admirably. However, you can still supply what I call the one-off or 'ad hoc' current awareness.

This type of current awareness works best in the smaller firm or dedicated practice area of a large firm where the information staff work closely with the lawyers and are aware of the projects or deals in which they are currently involved.

Ad hoc current awareness works like this:

- A group of lawyers may be setting up a deal with a particular company and you spot a significant item of news about the company in the press and notify them accordingly.

- One of the partners is preparing a speech to be delivered at a conference and you see a journal article on the subject of his proposed speech and alert him to its existence.

- You know that a senior lawyer is interested in a particular area of the law and you come across a conference on that very topic and inform him of its existence.

In order for ad hoc current awareness to be effective, you must draw your items of interest from sources which you know that your lawyers are unlikely to come across in the normal course of their work. The method of delivery of these hidden gems of information can be formal, i.e. via e-mail or internal memo, or informally, i.e. telling them in person.

Ad hoc current awareness is also effective because it is just that. It is tailored specifically to a particular lawyer's or group of lawyers' needs and its impact is doubled because it is unexpected.

The day before I wrote this part of the book, I supplied a piece of ad hoc current awareness to the group of lawyers with whom I work. In the course of checking over one of the external e-mail alerter services the firm subscribes to, I noted that a leading MP had mentioned at a conference that a major piece of legislation, which underpins all the work my lawyers do, was due to be reviewed at the end of the year. I could not recall seeing this titbit of news mentioned elsewhere and a quick search of a number of relevant sources confirmed I was right. A contact at the appropriate government department confirmed the nature of the review and I was also referred to a publication (which I would never have thought of consulting on the point) where I could find further information. I then prepared a short e-mail detailing my findings which I sent to all the lawyers in my group.

Team meetings

If you work in a small or medium sized firm or dedicated practice area in a larger one, you should make every effort to attend team and departmental meetings. Not only does it enable you to keep up to date with what the lawyers are currently working on and any developments there may be in the pipeline which could impact on the service you provide, but team meetings are an excellent way of promoting the information service. In recent team meetings at my own firm, I have reminded lawyers of the need to forward their know-how, provided tips on searching the Internet and recommended the best way to locate EU directives on the firm's intranet.

However many memos or e-mails you send out, however good your marketing literature is, however many tours of the library you run, it is often the chance remark in a specific context that has the most impact. Having reminded (diplomatically, of course) a partner at one of our team meetings that I could have quickly located the report that he failed to find for himself on a government website, he now routinely asks my advice on locating such reports on the Internet.

Reminding your users of what you can do and the services you provide can have beneficial knock-on effects. Initially, it may just be a request for an easy-to-find report, but I have often found this has the effect of the user saying: 'Well, if the information officer found that report for me, I wonder if he could track down this piece of information?' And word will spread too. Word of mouth recommendation is the best way of promoting your information department.

Training

Under this heading I shall look at ways of promoting your information service in the guise of training, that is educating your users about the firm's library, its resources and how to use them. I shall examine various ways of doing this: library tours, small group sessions, the formal presentation and one-to-one.

Library tours

This popular training standby serves to introduce users to the library service by showing them round the library, pointing out the stock and resources available, and perhaps explaining such administrative matters as opening hours, the procedure for issuing books and guidelines about photocopying.

I have always found such library tours to be pretty ineffective. They put me in mind of those groups of people on guided tours of country houses and stately homes. Those at the back of the group cannot always hear what is being said or see clearly what is being pointed out to them. The effect is similar with library tours – attendees come away with a vague, often confused, idea of what the library contains and the services it provides. However, if you are a keen advocate of the 'library tour' the following points might be worth bearing in mind.

Small groups

Keep each tour group down to a manageable number. I would recommend no more than five people in each group. This enables everyone to hear what is being said and see what is being pointed out to them. People are also less likely to be inhibited about asking questions if they are part of a smaller group. In a large busy working library, it is less distracting for the users (particularly if your library is used as a study area) to have a number of small groups being shown round rather than one large one.

Do not overload tour attendees with information but provide salient points about each section of the library's stock as you come to it. For example, at the reference section, you may point out a useful directory of law firms; at the book section, you could refer to one or two major texts and explain the process for issuing books. Stopping at the periodicals section would provide you with the opportunity to explain the circulation policy for journals and photocopying guidelines. If there are walk-up PCs you can point out the various databases that have been loaded on them and the data they contain.

Do not rush the tour – take your time and encourage questions. Always have a printed library guide which you can hand out at the conclusion of the tour.

Library guide

Many of the points I made about clarity in the section on writing abstracts are applicable when preparing a library guide whose contents might include:

- location of the library, its opening hours and how to contact staff;
- description of the book stock;
- how the material is arranged;
- the know-how classification scheme;
- list of journal titles held;
- services offered: research, database training, current awareness publications;
- procedure for borrowing books.

If library tours are arranged as part of the induction programme for new trainees then you have a particular target group and can design your tour accordingly. As trainee solicitors usually undertake a good deal of legal research, your tour can concentrate more on those databases which are available on lawyers' PCs.

Presentations and seminars

The thought of getting up and speaking in front of a group of people can be a daunting prospect for many – it really is a case of 'feel the fear and do it anyway'. However, it does get easier the more you do it.

The following is a list of tips which may go some way to calming those butterflies:

- Remember that you are the expert, you know what you are talking about, you are the authority on your subject.

- Prepare yourself thoroughly beforehand. Even if you have typed out what you intend to say, try not to deliver it as though you were reading from a script. As your confidence grows, you will find that you only need to note down bullet points on a series of 5" × 3" cards and you can use them as prompts or reminders of what you intend to say.

- Check out the venue in which you will be giving your talk. If you are going to be using equipment such as a microphone or a computer, make sure you know how to use them.

- If you cannot rehearse in the venue itself, rehearse the presentation in your head as though you were watching a movie.

- If your talk is accompanied by slides or a PowerPoint presentation, make sure that what you say is synchronised with the appropriate text on the slide. You can mark the points in your script at which you need to call up the next slide or line of text.

- If you are giving a slide presentation, always provide the text of the slides as handouts for your audience.

- Do not speak quickly. Nerves speed up people's speech patterns so pace yourself at normal conversational level; consciously adopt a more measured delivery.

- Do not avoid eye contact with your audience but do not focus on one person as they will become paranoic. Make eye contact with different parts of your audience.

- Make time for questions afterwards and try and anticipate what may be asked. If you do not know the answer to someone's question, it is better to say that you will contact them later (and make sure you do!) rather than give an inaccurate reply at the time thus creating a bad impression with your audience.

Your audience

Whatever kind of training you provide, whether it be a tour of the library, a formal presentation or one-to-one tuition, it is important to consider who your audience is and design your talk accordingly. They could be trainee solicitors new to the firm or qualified solicitors joining from other firms or organisations, or they could be secretaries or other support staff. It is no good, for example, concentrating on updating statutory instruments if your audience consists of secretaries.

One-to-one training

The availability of so many resources on lawyers' desktop PCs does provide the information officer with some excellent training opportunities. In a one-to-one situation, you can set the pace according to the needs and interests of the person you are assisting. The session can range from a ten minute tour round the firm's intranet to a half hour exploration of legal websites.

One of the most powerful weapons at your disposal in your marketing armoury is yourself. You may have such a small department that library tours are not feasible, or that getting a group of lawyers together to make a presentation is proving difficult to arrange, or that the facilities for doing so are simply not available. In the medium-sized firm or dedicated practice area, there are a number of ways you can still market the information service (and yourself) at the same time.

Above all, be proactive. Do not wait for lawyers to come to you, go to them. We could all end up simply e-mailing each other and never making any personal contact at all. From time to time, for example, personally deliver journal articles and caselaw rather than putting them in the internal post.

Nurture new joiners. Send them your 'library guide' or a brief introductory e-mail welcoming them to the firm and then follow it up after a couple of days by introducing yourself to them. If they require any assistance using databases or finding their way round the firm's intranet, now is the time to provide some dedicated one-to-one training before they start getting really involved in fee-earning work and have less spare time at their disposal.

Encourage the reluctant or infrequent user of your information services. There may be good reasons why their usage is infrequent – their work is of a nature that does not require a large research input, or they are pretty clued up about finding what they want themselves. They may even be shy of asking you (yes, there are shy lawyers!) or unwilling to admit their lack of knowledge on a particular subject.

Their reply to your casual enquiry, when you encounter one of your reluctant users by chance at the coffee machine, about what they are currently working on may prompt you into offering assistance. The reluctant user informs you that he is drafting a legal opinion and has been told that an unreported case neatly covers one of the points he is trying to make but he has been led to believe that it is very difficult to get hold of unreported cases. You point out that this is not always so and if he provides some details you will see what you can do. And, of course, you find the case for him. One reluctant user has been 'won over'.

Look for marketing opportunities. A chance remark from one of the secretaries in my department that she had trouble locating material on the firm's intranet led to a series of one-to-one training sessions with a number of secretaries not only in finding their way round the intranet, but searching on the Internet generally.

It is no good telling people what you can do and how you can assist them in your day-to-day role unless you actively demonstrate it by seizing those opportunities where you can market both yourself and your department.

4

Research and enquiries

Research and enquiry work is, arguably, the most interesting aspect of an information professional's role and the main reason why many people choose an information career. It is the public face of any library and information department and often the one aspect of the service by which user satisfaction is measured, so it is essential to get it right.

Basic facts about enquiries

Who asks the questions?

In a law firm, enquiries will come not just from the partners, lawyers and trainees but from anyone who works in the firm including support staff, secretaries and IT specialists. In certain circumstances, you may also receive enquiries from external sources such as information officers in other law firms.

What types of questions get asked?

They will range from the 'quick and dirty', i.e. those requiring an easy-to-find answer and very little research time and effort, to the in-depth requests which may take several hours or even days to complete.

What is the subject matter of the questions?

Many will be of a legal nature, but you may also get enquiries which come under the heading of 'business information'. Here are some examples of both types:

- *Legal enquiries*:
    - transcript of a case;
    - EU (European Union) legislation;
    - case law heard under a particular section of a statute.
- *Business information*:
    - background news stories on a particular company;
    - market and industry information;
    - statistics.

What are the ways in which enquiries are received?

There are three main ways in which enquiries are received:

- in person;
- over the telephone;
- in writing, e.g. memo, letter, e-mail, fax.

It could be assumed that an enquiry received by telephone would be more urgent than one received in writing, but in my experience this is not always so.

The way the enquiry reaches the person who is going to deal with it merely depends on the personal preference of the enquirer, though I have noted that, where it is available, e-mail seems to have replaced the telephone as the preferred method of delivering an enquiry.

The question of whether you should respond to the enquirer via the method you received the enquiry (e.g. answer a telephone enquiry with a telephone answer) depends on the nature of the answer to the question. If you have undertaken a good deal of research which requires a summary of the sources you have used, then it is clearly better to communicate that information in writing rather than over the telephone.

What does the enquirer really want?

Before actually starting to research the enquiry you have received, it is essential that you fully understand what you are being asked.

It is essential that you carry out what is called a 'reference interview' whereby you elicit from the enquirer exactly what it is he requires. Carrying out a successful reference interview enables you to focus your search strategy precisely and can save you wasted time and effort undertaking fruitless areas of research.

Undertaking a reference interview is more straightforward if you receive the enquiry in person or by telephone, but it should also be carried out if the enquiry is a written one where perhaps the enquirer has not expressed his thoughts clearly. You will still need to contact the enquirer for clarification.

I think the best way of demonstrating the usefulness of a good reference interview is to apply it to specific examples as shown below. For the purposes of this exercise I am disregarding the method by which the enquiry was received.

'Can I have a copy of the case X v Y?'

This is a straightforward question, but you could ask whether a hard copy is required or whether the enquirer would prefer to receive an electronic copy as an e-mail attachment.

'I remember seeing something recently about a new report on European hedge funds. Could I have a copy please?'

This is full of traps for the unwary. If you are up to speed with keeping up to date with new publications in those areas in which your lawyers practise, then you may already be aware of the report which is being referred to and you may even have a copy of it on order. If you do, you can pass this information on to your enquirer and he will be suitably impressed and tell his colleagues what a wonderful job you are doing. However, assuming that you do not know what report he is talking about, you must prise some more information out of him to help you track it down.

'Seeing something recently'

If he cannot recall the precise source, are there any publications or news services he looks at regularly where he might have come across it? Can he recall whether he saw it in a journal or a newspaper? What does he mean by 'recently'? (One person's idea of 'recent' is a week ago, another's is six months.)

'European hedge funds'

The word 'European' provides some clues: is it perhaps a report produced by the European Commission in Brussels or is it something produced by consultants or a financial institution that specialises in hedge funds?

'Could I have a copy'

Make it absolutely clear that the enquirer needs a copy of the actual report rather than the news item in which the report was mentioned. A small point maybe, but an important one. You might have gone to the trouble of purchasing a copy of the report when all that was required was a copy of the original news item.

Following your reference interview, the enquirer replies that he is pretty sure he saw it mentioned in an e-mail news bulletin that is circulated regularly by the information officer and that it was no more than a month ago. Armed with this extra information, you can now start your search for the report.

'I need some background information on the company Smith & Co.'

This is a very open-ended question: what does the enquirer mean by 'background information'? Does he just require basic directory information such as address, directors' details and summary financial data? Perhaps he needs the latest annual report or some news stories from the press? After a brief discussion, it is ascertained that the enquirer would like the company's entry from a directory of companies plus a news search going back over the past month.

You should always terminate a reference interview by agreeing on a timescale within which the results should be delivered to the enquirer.

If you don't know, ask!

Your enquirer may use a concept or idea that you have not come across before. You can always look this up in an appropriate source, but there is no harm in asking your enquirer during the reference interview what he means. I have found that lawyers are always happy to share their knowledge with you.

The search strategy

Once the reference interview is over and you have established exactly what it is your enquirer wants, you are now ready to formulate a search strategy. (Obviously, you do not need to do this for those straightforward 'quick and dirty' enquiries but it is useful to undertake this exercise if you are doing a research type of enquiry.)

Make a list of the sources you intend to consult on a sheet of paper and work through them one by one. Think of all the sources available to you in-house: books, journals, databases, the Internet. Once you have finished researching a particular source you can add any comments or observations arising as a result of that search, e.g. 'only a few articles found, none of any real value'. As you progress your research, further possible sources will occur to you.

Going that little bit further

If you are engaged on a piece of in-depth research over a number of days, you may get to the point when you have consulted all the sources on your strategy list and have found little or nothing on the topic under investigation.

This may well be the point at which to call a halt and acknowledge that perhaps there is nothing publicly available on the subject, or if there is, it is going to be very difficult to track down.

However, you could revisit your search strategy and see if there are any other sources you could try. As you have probably exhausted all *internal* sources, it is now time to examine external ones and this is the opportunity to really brainstorm, think laterally and come up with some ideas. You may also have to think beyond just *published* sources and consider, for example, contacting people. The following ideas might be worth exploring:

■ Are there any experts at universities who are specialists in their field and may have unpublished material on the subject?

■ Are there any organisations, associations, consultancies or specialist libraries that deal with the subject and which could be approached for assistance?

■ Have there been any conferences or seminars held on the subject?

Each of these approaches has their plus and minus points.

People

Contacting a person for assistance can sometimes have beneficial results. The expert in a particular field may be flattered to have been approached and be prepared to help; on the other hand, he may resent being contacted out of the blue by a stranger. It really is a matter of the 'luck of the draw' which attitude you come up against. In any event, it is vital that before contacting someone in this way that you really have done your research and ensured that there is no easily available published information on the subject.

It is advisable to briefly acquaint 'the expert' with the research you have done so far and ask him whether he is aware of any other sources or avenues that you could explore. This demonstrates that you have been thorough and is more likely to make the expert favourably disposed towards you. Nothing causes more annoyance than being cold called by someone who has done little or no preparatory work whatsoever and who then expects the expert to do all the work for them. If as an information officer you ever do adopt this approach, I suggest that the information profession is not for you.

It should also be borne in mind that if the expert is a lecturer at a university and does have unpublished information on the subject, he might be reluctant to release it (for example, he is writing a book on the subject).

Specialist libraries

It need not be assumed that you have to work in London to use the many specialist (legal and non-legal) libraries that are situated there. Many of the libraries which are attached to professional bodies (e.g. the Law Society, the Chartered Insurance Institute, the Royal Institution of Chartered Surveyors) offer enquiry and research services usually on a paid-for basis which are available to researchers via telephone, e-mail or letter. The London-based information professional has the benefit of using these libraries for personal research, but many of them do restrict access to 'non-members' so do not assume that you can simply walk in off the street. Some of the larger public libraries in the UK offer a 'business information service', again on a paid-for basis.

Conferences and seminars

Conferences and seminars are a useful source of 'hidden' information in that they represent current thinking and the speakers are (or should be) experts in their fields. Many conference organisers recognise the value of the information contained in conference proceedings and will charge a premium rate for the material. On the other hand, many published conference proceedings consist merely of the text of slides and have little value without the presenter's accompanying speech.

I am not advocating that you should use any of these suggestions whenever you need to expand your original search strategy and circumstances such as time and cost will make implementing many of them impracticable, but they do serve to give the researcher an idea of how he can really think round a research question and come up with a wide range of possible sources to explore.

Evaluating and analysing the information

There is a certain reluctance on the part of some information professionals to evaluate and analyse the information they have discovered in the course of their research. They are almost frightened to make a choice of material of behalf of the enquirer.

In most cases, though, it is necessary to undertake some kind of selection process. If your enquirer has asked you to supply him with about a dozen articles that have appeared in the last six months on a particular topic and your database search has thrown up 112, then you are certainly going to have to do some 'evaluating' to narrow the number down to the required dozen. If your enquirer has just two hours to go through material before he attends a meeting, then he will not be best pleased if you hand him 50 pages of printed text to absorb.

There is also the question of 'information overload' to be considered. Everyone nowadays is bombarded with too much information. An essential aspect of the information professional's role is to sift, filter and evaluate information and deliver high-quality, reliable data to the enquirer who wants to be assured that what is being given to him is the best of what is currently available.

Evaluation guidelines

The following are some guidelines on how to pick the best of a crop of articles and news items retrieved during the course of an online database search:

- Beware of headlines that promise a lot and deliver little. Newspaper headlines are designed to catch the reader's eye and encourage him to read the rest of the item the actual content of which does not always stand up to scrutiny.

- Scan the article. Is it well laid out with subheadings which lead the eye from one section to the next? Is it actually saying *something* or is it just waffle? You do not necessarily have to understand every concept put forward in the article so long as you have an understanding of the article's general thrust.

- How often do keywords associated with the subject appear in the course of an article? Most database searches can be set up so that only those articles where the search terms appear 'at least' a certain number of times are retrieved.

- How soon does it take for the article to get going? Do the first two paragraphs form a strong opening after which it tails off?

- For the lengthier type of article, is there a concise abstract summarising the content? Is there a bibliography?

- A database will often load what may seem, at first, to be duplicate news items. But the second item may be from a later edition and contain additional details that were not supplied in the first item. Does the second edition item contain information that contradicts what the first edition item says, e.g. a different statistic? It may be advisable in such a case to supply the enquirer with the items from *both* editions.

Know your sources

Successful research is as much about knowing your sources and potential sources as knowing about the subject matter itself. Often during the course of a reference interview, you may well be making assumptions to the enquirer about possible sources that you will be using. Knowledge of sources and potential sources comes with experience built up on the job. If you have worked on a particular topic before and know that there is very little published on the subject, you can mention this to your enquirer at the reference interview stage, but assure them that you will double check anyway. Something may have been published since you last did a similar enquiry!

You should also be broadening your range of source knowledge 'off the job' when you are not doing enquiries. When shelf tidying, take a few minutes to browse textbooks or reference works. Have a look at the contents list, scan the index, get a feel for the book's coverage and scope. Reference works in particular are notorious for containing 'hidden' gems of information (usually in an appendix) which, while not concerned with the actual subject matter of the book itself, are related to its main topic in some way.

Apply the same techniques to a journal: look at the types of articles it contains. Are they short newsy items or more considered longer pieces? Are case summaries provided? Is the coverage confined to the UK or is it more international in scope?

When you have a few minutes to spare, surf the Internet for sites of relevance to the types of enquiries you are getting or examine more closely those you have already come across. Look at the site's home page, check links and the structure of the site to ascertain where other useful data may be found. Remember, too, that an Internet site will be constantly evolving and changing as new data is added, so you need to check it regularly or sign up for the site's e-mail alerter service which notifies you when new information is added (assuming that the site offers this facility).

It would be impracticable to 'surf' an online database like Factiva or Lexis to get a feel for its content in the same way as you would an Internet site as you may be paying for the time you are online, though if you have paid a lump sum up front for unlimited access, this will not be so much of a consideration. However, database providers do produce hard-copy guides to their databases and you should study these to gain an idea of the range of sources covered and the search strategies required as each database will have its own idiosyncrasies and search techniques. Sign up for any training programme the database provider runs or arrange for some one-to-one training at your own desk.

Presenting the results

If you have been researching a particular subject for an enquirer, you may well have got together a number of articles photocopied from journals as well as items downloaded from an online database. Full bibliographical details (i.e. journal name, volume, number, date of issue and pagination) should be supplied for each journal article and, similarly, if any photocopied extracts are supplied from books, the title, author and date of publication should be clearly marked on the top page of the photocopy. It is always helpful to include an accompanying note drawing attention to the one article that covers the topic particularly well or to highlight that part of the article or book which is particularly relevant.

Sometimes there just isn't an answer!

Even in today's information-rich world there will be occasions when you are unable to locate the information that has been requested, maybe because there is nothing available on the topic or perhaps it cannot be released for reasons of confidentiality.

It is always advisable in these cases to prepare a short memorandum for the enquirer detailing the sources you have consulted as well as any external libraries you used or telephone calls you made in pursuit of the information. It is not merely enough to say that you have been unable to find anything – you need to demonstrate the thoroughness of your approach.

Signposter or facilitator?

In my experience, the information professional who deals with research and enquiries falls into one of two categories: he is either a 'facilitator' or a 'signposter'.

The facilitator will find the answer to the question on the enquirer's behalf; the signposter will merely point the way referring the enquirer to sources where the answer may be found.

I believe that the information professional who is truly 'professional' will always be a facilitator. To me the signposting role is a very frustrating one. How do you get to know your stock if you do not actually use the material to find the answers to questions? How can you recommend a book if you have never opened it? How do you build up knowledge of a subject matter if you never actually *research* the topic?

And yet I have worked with a number of signposters in the information profession who are happy with this approach to research and enquiry work and see nothing wrong in it. Unfortunately, this can lead to a reference and enquiry service where the standards of service fluctuate wildly depending on whether a facilitator or a signposter happens to be on duty on the enquiry desk.

However, there are certain circumstances in which it is necessary and prudent to be a signposter. I am thinking particularly of the interaction between the legal information officer and the trainee solicitor. A major part of the role of a trainee solicitor is 'legal research' which he will, usually, have been asked to do by his supervising lawyer or partner. In this instance, your role will be more of an advisory one, suggesting sources and search strategies.

Final words on research

- If you find you are getting stuck on a certain aspect of your research, take a break from it. If the deadline permits, sleep on the problem and come back to it the next day. The subconscious often sorts out difficulties and what seemed an intractable problem the day before will appear straightforward the next morning.

- If it is taking longer to deal with the enquiry than you originally anticipated, it is courteous to keep your enquirer informed of any possible delays to the deadline that was originally agreed upon.

- Do not assume there is nothing published on the subject until you have satisfied yourself that there is not. You must have explored all possible sources of information (both internal and external) and covered all eventualities. As you hone your research skills, it becomes easier to assess whether there is going to be much published information on a subject. Research has its own momentum: if the information is out there, the sources and leads will emerge during the course of the research process.

5

The Internet: threat or opportunity?

The development of the Internet, or World Wide Web, during the 1990s has dramatically raised the profile of the information profession. Anyone with access to a PC can now log on and search a vast range of sources. Suddenly, searching for information has become 'sexy'. Access to the Internet is everywhere: in the office, at home, in Internet cafés and shops, in libraries, in street booths – even the Greek island where I spend my annual 'chill-out' week now boasts its own Internet café.

The irony is, of course, that the Internet is not a sophisticated tool, but it has quickly become an indispensable part of everyday life worldwide and used with caution can be a valuable addition to the armoury of sources available to the information professional.

As the Internet is developing and changing so rapidly, seemingly on a daily basis, I have concentrated more in this chapter on the broad concepts and ideas associated with searching rather than specific points. There are plenty of books and courses available on searching the Internet which I would advise you to investigate if you wish to develop your web searching skills further.

Glossary

Let us start by explaining some of the jargon:

Browser: A program which allows a person to read hypertext, e.g. Internet Explorer is a browser.

Cache: A snapshot of a page when a spider (see below) crawled the web since which time text on the page will almost certainly have changed unless the site is rarely updated.

Favourites: If you come across a website or page that you like and will want to access regularly, you can add it to a list of favourite sites by clicking the 'Favorites' button on the toolbar of your browser, so it is easy to open them in the future without the need to type in the URL (see below). Some pages saved as favourites may display the text of the page at the date it was saved as a favourite. In order to reflect subsequent textual changes you must press the 'refresh' icon on your toolbar.

Hyperlink: A link from one document to another or to another place in the same document, indicated on screen by the text being in a different colour from the rest of the document, or by being underlined, or both.

Hypertext: A collection of documents containing hyperlinks.

Metasearch: Searches across a number of search engines at the same time.

PDF: Portable Document Format – a method for distributing information electronically which retains all the formatting and fonts of the original copy.

Search tools: A means of finding information on the Internet. There are two types of search tool: directories and subject listings (e.g. Yahoo! (*http://www.yahoo.co.uk*)) and search engines (e.g. Google (*http://www.google.co.uk*)), though many search engines also have subject listings. The term 'search engine' now seems to be in common usage to denote both types of search tool, but, strictly speaking, such usage is incorrect. Search engines use automated programs known as spiders to crawl the web looking for pages and text to index.

URL: Uniform Resource Locator – the address used on the web. Typically, an address will consist of a host name and a domain name. The host name is the unique name by which a site is known and the domain name is a group of sites whose host names share a common suffix. For example, in the URL *http://www.bbc.co.uk*, the host name is 'bbc' and the domain name is 'co.uk'. Every URL starts with 'http' (Hypertext Transfer Protocol) but you can usually omit this when typing the URL into the address field at the top of your browser.

WWW: World Wide Web, commonly known as 'the Web'. It is not a synonym for the Internet but is a subset of it. However, the terms 'the Web' and 'the Internet' have become interchangeable in common parlance. (The Internet is the actual network of networks where all the information resides.)

Search engines/directories

The key to searching the Internet is the search engines. Most people end up using the search engine that seems to deliver the best results for most of the searches they undertake. Or you may find, with experience, that you have a preference for one particular search engine based on how the search results are displayed or the 'look and feel' of the site. I would recommend that all Internet users check out Danny Sullivan's website SearchEngineWatch.com (*http://www .searchenginewatch.com/*) which provides advice on the various search engines' capabilities as well as tips on searching the Web.

However, it is best not to be over-reliant on one particular search engine and I suggest you get to know the capabilities of at least three. If anything, this will demonstrate the vagaries and inconsistencies of the Web – doing a search on the same topic on three different search engines often yields results ranked differently with some hits on one search engine not appearing on others.

In many cases, it is preferable to use a subject-dedicated directory as this will ensure that your results will be focused and relevant. One of the best known search directories for the legal sector is Lawcrawler (*http://lawcrawler.findlaw .com/*). An excellent starting point for any legal research on the internet are the portals maintained by Delia Venables (*http://www.venables.co.uk/*) and Sarah Carter (*http:// library.kent.ac.uk/library/lawlinks/default.htm*).

Each search engine, or directory, usually has its own on-screen guidance under such headings as 'Advanced searching' or 'Preferences'. It is therefore possible to restrict your search by date and place, or to use Boolean operators and other devices such as speech marks ("......") and symbols such as the plus or minus signs to focus your search, just as you would with conventional online searching.

In the list of results or 'hits' that are displayed as a consequence of your search, it is unwise to assume that the first item on the list is always going to be the most relevant. Search engine hosts are coy about the precise methods they use to rank results, but factors such as how many of the search terms were found in the document and their proximity to each other will have been taken into account.

Each result will contain an extract taken from the site which you can then hyperlink to. It is sometimes difficult to judge the relevancy of a page from these summaries as they have been lifted verbatim from the site and the context in which your search term happens to appear may not be very meaningful. Further information can be gleaned from the URL which appears below the extract; for example, in the domain name section 'ac' means the site is hosted by an academic institution, 'com' is a large global commercial entity and the country of origin is designated by universally accepted codes so that, for example, 'de' refers to Germany and 'fr' to France.

Can I rely on the information?

Once you start checking the sites generated by your search, there are two important points to consider: authority and currency. Look for a date when the site was created or updated; be careful though – sites prominently display the date of *access* on their front page rather than the date a document was published or created. Bear in mind too that although a document may have been *loaded* onto the site on a certain date it may have been published months before.

Next, try to ascertain who owns or has developed the site. In many cases, you will have gleaned this knowledge from the URL mentioned in the results list, but often you are linked directly to a document. How do you check that this document is from a bona fide source? It is time to 'climb the tree'! (I came across this phrase in Paul Pedley's book *The Invisible Web*[1] and it describes the process admirably.) You will have noticed that the URL is composed of several components separated by a forward slash; a (fictional) URL may therefore read as *http://www.abc.co.uk/def/ghi*. Climbing the tree involves deleting each successive part of the URL starting from the end and working your way towards the beginning of the address.

In the example *http://www.abc.co.uk/def/ghi*, first delete 'ghi' and then 'def' to reveal the next section or page, so that you should eventually get to the opening page of the site. Hopefully, this will be the area that contains the information on authority and validity that you are looking for. It may be a company name and logo or the name of the webmaster. Do not be distracted by images and slick design – assess the viability and usefulness of the site in the same way that you would for any information source, whether hard copy or electronic.

Sometimes, your progress up the tree is blocked as you encounter error messages or are denied access to pages but it is still an exercise worth pursuing. It is extremely easy for anyone to set up a website and post information and you need to ensure that the statute you have located has been put up by a reputable source and not by someone with a grudge who has tampered with the text and changed its meaning.

Using the Internet for research: for and against

For

■ The World Wide Web certainly lives up to its name – worldwide. Its coverage is global and is an absolute boon for any researcher based in the UK who has to look for non-UK material.

■ It is particularly good for the legal researcher – there is an incredible amount of legal information on the Web, particularly originating from the USA.

■ Serendipity: I am continually surprised at what can be found on the Web. For example, many offshore jurisdictions, often regarded as secretive, put up their regulations and statutes on the Web.

■ Browsing: surfing the Web can lead you down some interesting byways enabling you to light upon some fascinating nuggets of information.

■ The language of the Internet is English – many sites originating in countries outside the UK have an English language version as well as a version in the language of the original country.

■ The Web is carving a niche for itself as a primary source of information in subjects which, because of their intrinsic nature, are well suited to the medium of the Internet, a good example being archive television.

■ The Internet is useful for finding your way into an area of research with which you may be unfamiliar. If I am presented with a concept which is new to me, I will enter the terms into a search engine in order to get a quick understanding of what the subject is about which will, hopefully, give me some pointers as to the direction my research strategy should take me.

■ When the Web does not provide exactly what is required it often provides clues or signposts to where the information may actually be found, perhaps by contacting a real person or accessing a hard-copy source.

Against

■ The Web can be infuriatingly slow.

■ URLs change and you suddenly find you cannot access a site you have saved in your list of favourites. Even a minor change in the configuration of a URL will render it inaccessible.

■ The Web can be frustrating – pages become unavailable, internal error messages come up and sites disappear.

■ Webmasters revamp and relaunch their websites thereby altering the layout. That handy list of reports to which you frequently referred has been moved to another part of the site.

■ Sites may not be easy on the eye – they may be filled with distracting images, graphics and advertisements.

- The Web is a great timewaster. I advise the lawyers with whom I work not to spend too much time looking for information on the Web. If you have not found what you want in ten minutes, it is unlikely that you are going to find it on the Internet at all.

- It is often impossible to ascertain the date of documents found on the Internet. This is particularly worrying if your research involves statistics. I got quite excited when I searched the Web for house prices in an area where I intended to buy and found details of properties which appeared to be bargains until I realised I was looking at pages that were two years out of date. My advice is not to rely on the Web for statistics unless you can guarantee they are from a reputable source and are clearly dated. If you are in any doubt at all of their veracity, do not use them.

- Many companies and organisations see the Web primarily as a marketing tool and its research potential as very much a secondary concern. This attitude manifests itself in the design of companies' websites with their emphasis on fonts, colours, graphics and images to convey an impression about their organisation and its products. Research papers and documents which could be of interest to the information professional are often to be found further on in the site.

- A company is able to put procedures in place to monitor who is accessing their website, so if you are researching a company and there are questions of confidentiality, it is best to check with your enquirer whether you can access their website or not.

The invisible Web

The major drawback with the Internet is that search engines can only retrieve a small percentage of sites on the Web. First, there are the logistics of simply keeping up with the phenomenal growth of the Internet – 7.3 million new pages are added each day[2] – and second, the spiders take a snapshot (a 'cache') of a website on a particular date which could have been days, weeks or even months beforehand. Before the spider next visits the site, there may have been new data added so there will be a delay before the search engines can index the new information. Search engines and the spiders are not configured to deal with sites that are frequently updated.

The spiders miss out on a lot of valuable sites for a number of reasons:

- Search engines cannot get into subject databases.
- The site may be password protected.
- A registration process has to be gone through to gain access to the site.
- The search engine does not recognise certain codes, e.g. Word files or newsgroups.

In a White Paper published in 2000, BrightPlanet estimated that this 'invisible Web' was over 500 times larger than the 'surface Web'.[3]

I have to say, though, that when I searched for half a dozen sites generally acknowledged to be part of the invisible Web I located all of them by using the Google search engine. Perhaps I was lucky in the sites I chose or maybe Google (which is regarded at the time of writing as being the most effective search engine)[4] has upgraded its indexing methodology to cover more of these previously hidden sites. For example, Google has an option to search on groups, an area which is perceived as being part of the invisible Web.

Whatever the reason, it is best to be aware of the concept of the invisible Web when searching the Internet.

Training

One of the easiest ways for the information professional to market his skills and expertise in any organisation is to provide Internet training. Not just to the lawyers either, the potential audience could consist of anyone who works in the firm and uses the Internet whether in the office or at home. It will be necessary to alter the emphasis of your training depending on whether you are dealing with a lawyer or a secretary.

Seize this opportunity to become your firm's Web guru! I have always found the most effective way of training users to search the Internet is in a one-to one situation, where particular interests and needs can be addressed and levels of competency taken into account. A typical training session could cover all the points discussed in this chapter:

- search engines;
- the Web's good points;
- the Web's bad points;
- the invisible Web;
- checking authority and currency;

- climbing the tree;

- how to construct a search.

Practical example of research

I will conclude this chapter by looking at an enquiry I dealt with by using the Internet. (All the websites in the following research strategy report were accessed and working during April 2003.)

I used the search engines AlltheWeb (*http://www.alltheweb.com/*), Google (*http://www.google.co.uk/*), Invisible Web (*http://www.invisibleweb.com/*) and LawCrawler (*http://lawcrawler.findlaw.com/*). In all, the research took me about two hours to complete (though not all at one sitting).

The remit is to find information on the insurance markets in the ten countries who are due to join the EU in 2004: Cyprus, the Czech Republic, Estonia, Hungary, Latvia, Lithuania, Malta, Poland, the Slovak Republic and Slovenia. Any additional information on the general economic background of each of these countries would be useful but not essential.

A search has been undertaken on the Factiva news database over the past twelve months but it has only yielded five items. It has been decided, therefore, to carry out a search on the Internet to see what that brings up.

Using the items retrieved from Factiva as a starting point, I noticed that one article mentions a reinsurance intermediary called Benfield having published a review of the Czech

Republic insurance industry in June 2002. I decided to begin my search by seeing if I could locate a copy of that report.

- Searched for 'Benfield+reinsurance' on Google. The seventh hit in the list of results referred me to Benfield's website but clicking on the link brought up a proxy error report.

- Referred back to the summary in the list and pasted in the URL in the address box and this brought up the home page for Benfield (*http://www.benfieldgroup.com/index .htm*).

- Clicking on a research icon brought up a list of reports including the one on the insurance industry in the Czech Republic.

- I also spotted in the same list a recently published report on the insurance industry in the Slovak Republic. Both reports were downloaded.

- I checked the authority of the site by looking at the section in which background information was provided on Benfield and as the two reports cited references and sources, I was more than happy with the authority and reliability.

- Going back to my Factiva articles, one mentioned a review of the Slovenian insurance market by the 'Insurance Information Institute Database'. Putting that phrase into the Google search engine brought up nothing.

- Using the same phrase, InvisibleWeb came up with the 'Insurance Information Institute Search' but the Internet connection was slow and I could not download the site.

- AlltheWeb did come up with the 'Insurance Information Institute' (*http://www.iii.org/*) but I could not see a search option on the home page. I tried linking to other parts of the site but connections were slow, so decided to try again later when, hopefully, conditions would be more favourable.

- I went back once more to the Factiva articles and noticed an 11 June 2002 item which said that Munich Reinsurance had produced a study on the candidate countries which showed that they offered lucrative prospects for the insurance industry.

- I accessed Munich Reinsurance's site (*http://www .munichre.com/default_e.asp*) via Google and, using the on-screen search option, I entered the term 'candidate countries' and found the report I wanted. It looks at insurance in Central and Eastern Europe generally and will provide useful background information. There are still eight countries left to research.

- Called up the 'Insurance Information Institute' website again to see if I would have more success at finding the report on the Slovenian insurance market on a second attempt. This time I found the search box but neither 'Slovenia' or 'Slovenian' produced any matches.

- I decided to see if any of the remaining eight countries had insurance associations as I thought they were more than likely to produce overviews of the insurance industries in their respective countries. I searched Google using the various countries' names with 'insurance' and 'association' as my search terms.

- One of the hits that came up was a reference to a 'List of Insurance Associations' provided by the East-West Management Institute, Inc. (EWMI) Budapest, whose home page (*http://www.ewmi.hu/*) informed me that they were 'committed to assisting economic reform in developing and transition economies'. The list supplied addresses and websites for all the remaining countries with the exception of Cyprus and Malta.

- Using the EWMI list, I checked the website of the Estonian Financial Supervisory Authority (English version) (*http://www.fi.ee/eng/index.html*) and found their *Insurance Yearbook 2001* which was printed in 2002 – a bit out of date, but further updates could always be obtained by contacting the authority itself.

- Next I looked at the Association of Hungarian Insurance Companies (English version) website (*http://www.mabisz .hu/english/index.html*) but was unable to download the latest version of their insurance yearbook. I tried the Hungarian Financial Supervisory Authority (*http://www .pszaf.hu/english/noflash.html*) but the only reports available were mainly of a broader economic nature so I took a note of the URL should the need arise to check them out later.

- Back to our list of insurance associations and this time I checked the Latvian Financial and Capital Markets Commission website (*http://www.fktk.lv/en/*). Although there was a promising list of reports under the heading 'Statistics', a quick perusal revealed that they were not of great relevance.

- The Lithuanian State Insurance Supervisory Authority website (*http://www.vdpt.lt/en/*) had a very good annual overview of the insurance industry.

- I also found useful reports for Poland from the Polish State Office for Insurance Supervision (*http://www.punu.gov .pl/index_eng.html*) and for Slovenia from the Slovenian Insurance Association (*http://www.zav-zdruzenje.si/E_info .htm*).

- I still needed to find something on Cyprus and Malta so decided to use LawCrawler. I entered the terms 'cyprus insurance market' in the search box and found a link to the Insurance Association of Cyprus (*http://www.iac.org.cy/*) which had details of a report which can be ordered.

- I used LawCrawler again, only this time the search terms were 'malta insurance market'. This got me several results, though no useful direct links. However, several mentioned the Malta Financial Services Authority and using Google I located their website (*http://www.mfsa .com.mt/mfsa/index.htm*), a search of which revealed a guide to insurance business in Malta dated October 2002.

Comments and observations

- Despite regarding myself as a seasoned web researcher, I was pleasantly surprised not only at the amount of information I found but also its quality.

- It was interesting to note that all of the insurance association websites had an English version as well as the one in the country's native language. English is indeed the language of the Internet.

- Even if I had not had the few clues thrown up by the Factiva news articles to start me off, I located good reports for both the Czech and Slovak Republics on their respective websites (*http://www.cap.cz/eindex.html*) and (*http://www.slaspo.sk/index_en.php?kategoria=10099*).

- Interestingly, though, I could not locate the Benfield report despite employing such search terms as 'insurance', 'market', 'report' and 'Czech' on a number of search engines – which just goes to prove that you cannot find everything on the Internet!

Conclusion

It is not unfanciful, I think, to regard the Internet's value as a research tool as being a metaphor for our increasingly 'dumbed-down' society. It lacks the structure and functionality of a commercial database such as Factiva or Lexis, especially with regard to indexing. Its most relevant hit in a list of results could be months out of date. It is a 'loose baggy monster' (you can do a search on the Internet to discover who originally coined that phrase) absorbing more and more data every minute of every day, only a proportion of which is searchable. It is, generally speaking, not effectively searched by the majority of people who access it. It can be unreliable, frustrating and downright annoying.

And yet, it has transformed the role of the information professional allowing him access to an incredible range of sources. It has gained a widespread acceptance and level of recognition in an amazingly short time. Everyone has heard of the Internet even if they have never used it.

There is a belief among employers who say that because everything is on the Web (a statement which is, of course, nonsense), there is no need to employ information professionals because the end user can find everything he wants for himself. This is a very shortsighted comment as my experience is that users do not often find the information they want on the Web or do not search it properly.

The widespread application of the Internet has provided wonderful opportunities for the information professional not just in the sense of widening the information resources at his fingertips, but also for enhancing his role in providing advice and training on searching the Web effectively.

Notes

1. Paul Pedley (2001) *The Invisible Web: Searching the Hidden Parts of the Internet*. Aslib-IMI.
2. 'The future just happened: black holes in cyberspace – the invisible web' (*http://news.bbc.co.uk/hi/english/static/in_depth/programmes/2001/future/invisible_web.stm*), accessed 27 January 2003.
3. BrightPlanet (2000) 'The deep web: surfacing hidden value', White Paper, BrightPlanet, July 2000, 41 pp. (*http://www.completeplanet.com/Tutorials/DeepWeb/index.asp*), accessed 12 April 2003.
4. SearchEngineWatch.com (*http://searchenginewatch.com/*) says Google is 'highly recommended as a first stop in your hunt for whatever you are looking for' (*http://www.searchenginewatch.com/links/major.html*), accessed 21 April 2003.

6

You say taxonomy, I say classification – you say thesaurus, I say classification

That traditional area of library science, classification, has undergone something of a reinvention in the electronic age. Now everyone in the information world refers to 'taxonomies' and 'thesauri' but the basic concepts are the same whichever term is used as can be seen from the following list of definitions which are taken from the *Oxford English Dictionary*.[1]

Classification
1. The action of classifying or arranging in classes, according to common characteristics or affinities; assignment to the proper class. 2. The result of classifying; a systematic distribution, allocation, or arrangement, in a class or classes; esp. of things which form the subject-matter of a science or of a methodic inquiry.

Taxonomy
1. Classification, esp. in relation to its general laws or principles; that department of science, or of a particular science or subject, which consists in or relates to classification; esp. the systematic classification of living organisms. 2. (With a and pl.) A classification of anything.

Thesaurus

1. A collection of concepts or words arranged according to sense. 2. A classified list of terms, esp. key-words, in a particular field, for use in indexing and information retrieval.

It is an irony that classification which is at the core of what an information professional does and is, arguably, the most valuable skill he can offer an employee seems to have had its importance downgraded over the years, certainly if the experience of recent library and information science graduates is anything to go by. Traditional cataloguing and classification skills do not seem to be taught on information management courses as much as they used to.[2]

If you have not had much experience of constructing a thesaurus or arranging subject terms in a coherent and meaningful order, either theoretically or practically, I suggest you seek out as many examples as you can find. They do not have to be law specific – any kind of classification system will do just so long as you get an idea of how a good scheme is put together.

The Internet is a good place to start. A brief outline of the Dewey decimal system, widely used in many UK public libraries, is available at *http://www.olcl.org/dewey/*. The BUBL Information Service (*http://www.bubl.ac.uk*) utilises Dewey as the organisation structure for its integrated interface to the subject gateways. The BLISS Classification Association (*http://www.sid.cam.ac.uk/bca/bcahome.htm*) promotes the development and use of the Bliss Bibliographic Classification (BC2).

However, many classification schemes are not really suitable for the types of libraries found in law firms. They are either too general and broad based like Dewey or their detail is not suitable for what can be very small collections. Many academic libraries with large law collections use BLISS or Moys.[3]

If you have a very small collection of books, say no more than two shelves worth, there is no reason why you should not just arrange your books in title or author (surname) order. Purists will probably throw their hands up in horror at such a suggestion, but if you are an information officer supporting a very specialised area of the law, and there are few relevant published titles or you have a small budget which restricts the number of books you can buy, it makes a lot of sense to do so.

Assuming that your book collection fills more than these two shelves, you will then need to think about using some classification scheme to arrange them.

The simplest scheme to adopt, widely used in law firms, is to classify books by broad legal subjects, e.g. criminal, contract, family, investment, insurance. There is no need to drill down further and subdivide those subjects into their constituent parts. Within each subject area, the books can be arranged on the shelves in order of author's surname.

The labels you attach to the spine of the book will therefore reflect the two criteria outlined above. Do not, for obvious reasons, attempt to write the full subject classification on the label but use easily recognised abbreviations, e.g. CRIM for criminal law and INS for insurance law. The following examples demonstrate what I mean:

Title: Criminal Evidence

Author: May, Richard

Classification: CRIM

Label on spine: CRIM/M

Title: Law of Insurance Contracts

Author: Clarke, M.A.

Classification: INS

Label on spine: INS/C

Constructing a classification scheme

This is where the fun really starts. The area where legal information professionals are likely to be called upon to construct a classification scheme or thesaurus is for an internal collection of know-how which usually consists of documents which focus on very specific legal points. Therefore the construction of a classification system to adequately reflect this complexity requires a good knowledge of the law and, very likely, a particular area of the law. Is an information professional the best person to tackle such a task?

If the information professional has legal as well as information qualifications then he is well placed to undertake classification construction. There may well be a case for getting a team together to work on it, a kind of thesaurus constructed by committee.[4]

But even if the information officer does not have much legal experience, the task, although daunting, can be made less so if certain points are borne in mind.

- Construct your scheme using the hierarchical concept:

    Level 1 term

        Level 2 term

            Level 3 term

            Level 4 term

- It is likely that your thesaurus will relate to one particular area of the law whose terms and concepts are becoming more familiar to you the longer you are in the post. Use textbooks or *Halsbury's Laws* to check on the meaning of terms and their place in a hierarchy.

- Your level 1 terms should reflect the nature and emphasis of the collection for which they are designed. If you have a lot of material on building societies, make that a level 1 term; otherwise if the amount of material you have in relation to material on other types of financial institutions is small, then make 'building societies' a second- or third-level term, and make financial institutions a level 1 term.

- Even if you regard your theoretical classification knowledge as 'sketchy', it is worth bearing in mind that you have the mindset of an information professional. You constantly retrieve material using a variety of classification schemes, you know that if you have located a subject in a document or on a database then it is likely you will have been led to it by a well constructed index.

- A major part of constructing a classification scheme is standardisation. At the simplest level, for example, is it going to be Tax or Taxation?

- Keep the concept of moving from the 'general' to the 'particular' in mind (e.g. Tax → Taxation systems → Europe → United Kingdom → Isle of Man).

- Design the structure in such a way so as to incorporate any future developments in the law.

- Could one term possibly be the subset of another? For example, is Building Societies going to be a level 1 term or would you prefer it to be a subset of Financial Institutions?

- Make a decision about countries. Should each country have a separate entry in the scheme or should it be a subset of a term? In other words will it be Germany → Taxation or Tax → Germany?

- Try not to mix subject terms with terms that represent *types* of material or the *sources* of material at the same level in your hierarchy. For example, you have chosen Tax as a level 1 term for your classification and you might choose Statutes (type) as a level 2 term and Inland Revenue Guidance Notes (source) as a level 3 term. Having all three terms, 'Tax', 'Statutes' and 'Inland Revenue Guidance Notes' as level 1 terms would throw up inconsistencies in the way the classification scheme was constructed. This would be reflected in the way the documents were physically arranged and be confusing to the users.

- Use *see* or *see under* to direct users to preferred terms.

There are a number of software programs on the market that specifically facilitate the classification/taxonomy/thesaurus design process.[5]

Cataloguing

Classification is closely associated with cataloguing (librarians of a certain generation refer to 'cat 'n' class') which is a process whereby books and other materials held in a library are described and indexed. Traditionally, libraries had their contents listed on catalogued cards which were filed in serried ranks of drawers. Nowadays, of course, the trend is for the library catalogue to be available in an electronic format.

If you want to get an idea of what catalogue records look like, many university libraries have their catalogues online or check out the British Library catalogue at (*http://blpc.bl.uk/*).

Creating catalogue records

Detailed cataloguing records such as you would find in an academic or national library's catalogue are inappropriate for a working law library.

Your book catalogue should incorporate, as a minimum, the following information:

- the title (and any subtitle) of the book, including any titles by which it might have been previously known, or any nickname by which it is commonly referred to by lawyers (e.g. the 'white book' or the 'purple book');
- the author(s) or editor(s) of the book;
- the publisher;
- the date of publication;
- the edition;

- the ISBN;
- the classification or shelf mark.

A record for a book might therefore look something like this:

Author: Clarke, M.A

Title: Law of Insurance Contracts

Edition: 4th

Publisher: LLP

Date of publication: 2002

ISBN: 1 84311 170 5

Shelved at: INS/C

It is also necessary to bear in mind the various ways in which a user might seek out a book:

- by author;
- by title;
- by nickname;
- by subject.

With the advent of online catalogues, the ways in which books can be retrieved have increased. There is usually an option to 'search everything' so books can be accessed, for example, by publisher or date of publication. The old card catalogue system was far more restrictive in that you were limited to searching by author (unless the book was commonly known by its title) or subject. A title search could only be done unless you first ascertained the classification number of its subject and then searched through all the records for that particular class mark.

Intranet

The other area where the information professional may be involved in classifying material is with regard to an intranet the firm has set up. An intranet can be defined as a 'private web' that can only be accessed by the employees of the organisation it serves.

An intranet can consist of the following mix of pages:

- websites;
- commercial databases that use web technology to transmit their data (an inclusion of this type of database on an intranet is normally subject to approval by the database provider);
- internal procedures and policies (how to apply for leave, health and safety issues, fire evacuation instructions);
- internal telephone directory;
- details of local counsel employed in the UK and overseas;
- guides on using databases;
- legal research guides;
- the nearest post office, bank, hairdresser, etc. to the firm.

In other words, your intranet can include virtually anything you want. Do not be constrained by what you already have in hard text; think of topics where it would be useful to collate the information and make it available to everyone in the firm (in the list above details of local counsel used and amenities near the firm are two good examples of this).

When putting together an intranet the most important consideration is not just to create direct electronic versions of the hard copy, but to rethink the material in visual terms and apply your ideas accordingly. For example, if you intend to post an internal telephone directory, include additional features such as a photograph of each staff member as well as a brief biography mentioning any areas of specialisation.

Making it easy for the user to find their way round your intranet should be a prime consideration, but in reality this is not always possible, as intranets grow and become unwieldy so that useful sites and information get tucked away. This is the main problem with every intranet I have seen. Scrolling down to read a long list of headings and text rendered in the smallest of fonts so that as many words as possible can be crammed onto the home page is a feature of many intranets.

It helps when designing an intranet to use the broad classification principles outlined earlier in this chapter, i.e. moving from the general to the particular using your level 1, 2 and 3 terms, in order to assist your users in finding the information they require.

The following are some points that you might like to consider when setting up an intranet.

- Who are the users going to be? Just the lawyers or everyone in the firm?
- Always be aware of the fact you are designing a *visual* information resource. Make links to other pages and documents as appropriate.
- Do not make the on-screen text too wordy as people will simply not read it. If you wish to load lengthy documents create them in PDF or Word format.

- Look at commercial Internet sites to get ideas and inspiration.

- Do not go overboard on different font sizes, colours and images as these can be distracting for the user.

The major concern with any intranet is keeping it up to date and there is really no point in contemplating launching one unless you can guarantee it will be constantly monitored for accuracy and relevancy. Too many people climb on the intranet bandwagon and set one up without careful planning and thought. It is probably a good idea to map out your proposed site on sheets of paper first before trying to convert it into screen format.

The other concern regarding a firm's intranet is who in the firm actually 'owns' it. As you will have seen from the typical list of pages that can be included on an intranet, it covers a range of departments and areas of interest and is in no way confined to the traditional information department. It is important that one person or group of persons should be designated as site editors in order to maintain consistency of approach and standardisation of terminology.

Intranet and web design is a new discipline to which information professionals can bring their traditional classification and indexing skills.

Notes

1. Online version *http://dictionary.oed.com/entrance.dtl*, accessed 26 February 2003.
2. The views of recent information graduates are examined in G. Sands (2002) 'Cat and class: what use are these skills to the new legal information professional?', *Legal Information Management*, 2(2), 19–22.

3. Elizabeth M. Moys (2001) *Moys' Classification and Thesaurus for Legal Materials*, 4th edn rev. and expanded. Munich: K.G. Saur.

4. This is what Christine Miskin and her colleagues did when they set up a taxonomy for the Legal Journals Index in 1986 – *see* Christine Miskin (1986) 'Taxonomies', *Legal Information Management*, 2(1), 16–23.

5. Miskin 'Taxonomies'; Liz Edols (2001) 'Taxonomies are what?', *FreePint*, 97, 4 October (*http://www.freepint.com/issues/041001.htm #feature*).

7

Know-how and knowledge management

Know-how

If you are a newcomer to the world of legal information, you may not have come across the concept of 'know-how' before, but you will quickly realise that it is a very important part of a firm's information resource; indeed, many lawyers will say that it is *the* most important.

Know-how, a term that has been in use for many years in legal information, can be defined as documentation generated within a law firm as a result of a deal or project undertaken by its lawyers. This documentation can include advice notes, reports, agreements, research notes, commentary on caselaw, counsel opinions and precedents. Generically, of course, it comes under the umbrella term 'information' but is distinguished by the fact that it is *internally* generated material.

The purpose of know-how is to make life easier for the lawyers in the firm: they can draw on previous knowledge and research without having to reinvent the wheel; they are able to conform to house-style when drafting a document – in effect, they can call on the collective expertise of the firm to make their job easier. I think lawyers like the idea that the information they are (re)using can be relied upon as having the authority of a colleague whom they can contact for further clarification (assuming that the lawyer still works for the firm). This is reassuring, particularly for the newly qualified lawyer who may be dealing with a topic that is new to him or outside his own particular specialisation.

In order to make the most effective use of know-how, it has to be arranged in such a way that it can be retrieved easily. Each item needs to be classified according to a predetermined indexing system and a concise summary of its contents prepared. (Information and advice on constructing a classification scheme for a know-how database and writing summaries can be found in Chapters 3 and 6.)

The typical collection in its hard-copy format could consist of A4 files arranged on the shelves, or, if space is a consideration, then in document wallets kept in a filing cabinet. Each file or folder will include a list of its contents including a summary of each item. Creating an electronic version of your files brings such additional benefits as word searching and links to the original document.

Whether your collection is in hard copy or electronic format it is important that it is clearly labelled and organised. Another important consideration is to ensure that if the material is of a confidential nature or that it should not be used without first consulting its author then a note to that effect should be attached to the document itself. Often a piece of advice may contain sensitive information relevant to a particular deal but the underlying concepts are of wider application.

In order to make a know-how collection truly valuable, I believe that it should consist solely of *internally* generated material. I am aware that many know-how collections do include material available in the public domain such as journal articles and company brochures, but, in my opinion, the inclusion of external documentation devalues the collection as a whole. There may be a case for including the odd article on a topic for which information is hard to find, but you could be infringing copyright anyway by including photocopied articles in your collection which are more than likely to be copied again because of their rarity value.

I can understand why some information officers would want to include this extramural material. Many lawyers do regard a firm's know-how collection as its major information repository and will assume that if there is 'nothing in know-how' then there is nothing on the subject anywhere. For example, in an environment where a number of databases are available on desktop PCs, lawyers may only search the know-how database (assuming it is searchable in electronic format) either through pressure of time, lack of knowledge of the required search strategies or laziness.

Readers may think that the most important aspect of a know-how system is creating the classification scheme by which the material is arranged. This is important, yes, but there is one overriding concern about any know-how system for any legal information officer and that is getting the material out of the lawyers in the first place.

I deliberately use the phrase 'getting out of' because the process does seem to be akin to extracting a bad tooth.

Although lawyers seem to favour know-how above all other information sources at their disposal, they are notoriously reluctant when it comes to actually donating items to the collection. Many lawyers like to hoard information for themselves to enable them to be the firm's perceived expert on a particular topic. This attitude need not necessarily be construed as a sign of insecurity on their part but merely a healthy business acumen. Fees are generated from providing advice to clients and if a lawyer can carve a niche for himself in an area of law where few of his peers specialise, so much the better for his kudos, career and fee-earning capacity. Then there is the simple matter of convenience. It is easier for a lawyer to get up and walk over to his own set of files on the shelves in his office rather than pay a visit to the information department. (I am aware that this argument loses validity where the firm has a know-how database in which the item can be accessed by clicking on an icon and opening up the document on a PC screen, but there is still a resistance to electronic delivery of information, particularly by some older lawyers.)

If, as information officer, one of your tasks is to extract know-how from lawyers, then your job will be made much easier if you have the support of the partners in the firm. If they can see the value of know-how and give a lead in contributing items to the system, then assistants and junior lawyers are more likely to follow suit. There has to be a culture of knowledge-sharing within the firm. Many firms, for example, include the extent of a lawyer's contribution to the know-how system as part of his annual appraisal.

Knowledge-sharing is a laudable aim but extremely difficult to put into practice. If you want to keep your know-how collection continuously refreshed with new material then as an information professional you must adopt all kinds of methods, both formal and informal, in order to cajole the material out of your lawyers. The following methods have all been used either by myself or colleagues in law firms:

- Set up a system whereby once a document, agreement or piece of advice has been finalised and approved you automatically receive a copy for inclusion in the know-how files (subject to any confidentiality considerations of course).

- Make sure you attend team and departmental meetings; if a deal is discussed ask the lawyer concerned to send you any know-how arising from that deal. Follow this up with an e-mail/telephone call or, even better, a visit to the lawyer's office to request a copy.

- Prepare a monthly summary of know-how added to the files and make sure contributors' names are prominent in order to act as an incentive to those colleagues who are reluctant to contribute anything. Send a copy of the summary to all lawyers as well as pinning a copy on noticeboards or the firm's intranet.

- Award a bottle of champagne to the lawyer who contributes most know-how over a certain time period (anything from one month to six months, depending on your generousity and your budget).

- If all the firm's documents are stored centrally in an electronic retrieval system (and here I mean a document management system rather than one designed specifically for information retrieval purposes) regularly search it for relevant items.

- If the lawyers in your firm or practice area produce regular summaries of work in progress make sure you receive copies so you can track the completion of deals and request any associated documentation.

- Just ask lawyers for know-how in the course of day-to-day business, by the coffee machine, when you deliver that urgent photocopy of a case, when they come into the information department (all these approaches would probably be more appropriate for the smaller firm).

Knowledge management

Another term you are certainly going to come across in the legal information world is 'knowledge management', a concept which has only really come to the fore in the late 1990s. The best definition of knowledge management I have come across is the one that I found on the Clifford Chance intranet: 'Knowledge Management, or KM, is the process by which a firm makes its collective knowledge accessible to each lawyer or other person who could benefit from it'.

What then is this 'collective knowledge' but the 'know-how' I have been discussing in the early part of this chapter? Lawyers and law firms have been involved in 'knowledge management' long before the term came into common usage. Unfortunately, it is a term which is misused by information professionals and nowhere more so than in the literature on the subject where 'knowledge management' is often confused with 'information management'.

In many cases anyway, the terms are synonymous: when does the 'knowledge' that resides in someone's head become 'information'? For instance, I know how to change the fuse in a plug because at some point I have been given the information that enables me to do it (whether orally by someone telling me or by my reading an instruction manual on wiring). That knowledge resides in my head and I may at some point pass that knowledge on to someone else. At what stage in this process does that knowledge transmute itself into information? I have never been asked by an enquirer if I have any knowledge on a subject, but I have been able to supply the *information* on a subject which fills the gaps in his *knowledge*.

The element of opinion or judgement is invariably an integral part of someone's knowledge; for example, I was once asked if any of the lawyers in the practice area I support could recommend a law firm in a particular jurisdiction. One lawyer was able to provide a name with the recommendation that they were a reliable, competent firm. The name of the firm could have been obtained from any commercial directory of law firms but in this case it was supplied with the additional personal knowledge that they were a competent firm.

If you were to take any article which discusses knowledge management and substitute the word 'information' for the word 'knowledge' wherever it occurs, I guarantee that in most cases, the meaning that the author is trying to convey would not be changed at all.[1]

Capturing the knowledge or know-how that resides in people's heads is all to do with ways of extracting that 'knowledge' and turning it into 'information' and the methods I have described above are some ways of doing that.

Note

1. This point is well made in T.D. Wilson (2002) 'The nonsense of "knowledge management"', *Information Research*, 8(1), paper no. 144, available at *http://InformationR.net/ir/8-1/paper144.html*.

8

Copyright

Copyright is a complex issue: I do not propose to go into great detail about copyright matters within the scope of this book but would advise any information officer to familiarise himself with the current situation by reading a book on the subject, attending a course or contacting CILIP (Chartered Institute of Library and Information Professionals). I shall be looking at the issue of copyright from the perspective of the information professional within a commercial profit-making organisation. There are other guidelines and regulations for libraries in the education sector or for organisations that are document delivery services.

The whole issue of copyright is a can of worms and the situation is made worse for information professionals who have to balance the right of copyright holders with the desire of users to have information delivered to them quickly and in the format they want.

All information professionals should be aware of copyright issues, but those working in the legal sector need to be doubly aware of them. You may be fortunate in having an intellectual property (IP) lawyer working in your firm to whom you can turn for advice, but the reality is that many information professionals are the first port of call when users want to know whether they are infringing copyright or not.

Where copyright applies

These are the areas where the information professional needs to consider copyright issues:

- photocopying newspaper and journal articles and distributing them internally;
- photocopying contents pages of journals and distributing them internally;
- downloading items from a commercial database or CD-Rom and distributing them internally either in hard copy or electronically;
- making PDF copies of newspaper and journal articles and distributing them by e-mail internally;
- photocopying sections of a book and distributing them internally;
- photocopying internal memos and agreements and distributing them internally;
- downloading and printing material from the Internet and distributing it internally;
- any of the above activities but distributing them externally, i.e. to people outside the firm, either in hard copy or electronically.

All of these activities, with the possible exception of photocopying internal memos and agreements, will be protected, to some extent, by copyright. Exceptions include very old material which is out of copyright. Some categories of rightsholders (e.g. the European Commission) also rarely enforce their rights. HMSO (Her Majesty's Stationery Office) permits unrestricted copying and reproduction of certain categories of Crown copyright material. A series of guidance notes have been posted on the HMSO website (*http://www.hmso.gov.uk/guides.htm*).

Copyright licences

An information professional needs to investigate taking out two licences to cover the photocopying of material that takes place within his firm – one for journals and books (the Copyright Licensing Agency) and the other for newspapers (the Newspaper Licensing Agency). If you operate, or are planning to operate, any kind of current awareness service which involves the copying of articles and distributing them within your firm, then you must familiarise yourself with any conditions laid down by either agency in the operation of such a service.

Having a CLA licence enables the items to be photocopied from certain specified journals (a list of these is maintained on the CLA website (*http://www.cla.co.uk*)). Although the terms of a licence may vary depending on the type and size of firm or organisation you work for, generally a licence will permit you to photocopy the following:

- one article from an issue of a periodical
- one chapter from a book
- one case report from published law reports
- or 5 per cent of the publication if greater than the above

for each single occasion or purpose, provided that the work is not listed in the excluded categories and excluded works list.[1]

A licence from the Newspaper Licensing Agency (their website is at *http://www.nla.co.uk*) permits photocopying and distribution of a wide range of UK newspapers. The number of copies made will depend on the agreement you have drawn up with the NLA.

Good practice

The important thing to remember about copyright is to ensure that you have covered yourself within the law and that the lawyers and other staff you support are aware of the guidelines and are seen to be operating within them. No information officer is going to put their hand on their heart and swear that no illegal photocopying takes place within their firm, but you can adopt some good practices which ensure that all employees are fully aware of what they are permitted to copy:

- Place notices by photocopiers explaining the limits on photocopying from books and journals. The CILIP, CLA and NLA all produce such notices. The CLA also produces a list of excluded publications from which photocopies cannot be made and this too should be displayed near photocopying machines.

- If you keep a journal title in your library that is on the CLA's excluded list, it might be a good idea to affix a note to the box in which the journals are stored explaining that under the terms of the CLA licence held by the firm, photocopying from that particular title is not permitted.

- Current awareness bulletins, particularly those sent by e-mail, should carry a rider explaining the limits within which the bulletin can be distributed. For example, if it can be sent on to clients and third parties outside the firm, then add some suitable wording at the beginning of the bulletin explaining that this can be done. If the suppliers of a bulletin have said that distribution should only be to employees within the firm or a particular branch of the firm, then make such a restriction explicit with the appropriate wording.

The problem with copyright matters is that so many areas are vague and open to interpretation and you may receive differing opinions from different practitioners. However, I think you should be particularly aware of situations where extracts from books, journals, databases or the Internet are copied and included in the text of handouts or information packs issued to external delegates who attend a conference or seminar at your firm's office. Photocopied texts should clearly state that they have been made in accordance with copyright regulations, or under the terms of the CLA licence, or with the permission of the owner of the website. You just never know who may be attending the conference.

Databases and CD-Roms

There is no blanket licence for electronic products. Information professionals must adhere to the agreement concluded with the provider of each database they subscribe to and ensure that the lawyers they support are aware of any conditions regarding downloading and sending information on to third parties.

The Internet

There is a perception held by many in the information and legal professions that any information posted on a website is in the public domain and that text can be copied without compunction. This view is a dangerous one. You should check any copyright notice posted on the website from which you want to copy text and, in the absence of one, contact the site owner or webmaster.

There is also the perception in law firms, and indeed any organisation, that so long as you are merely copying and distributing material internally, you have carte blanche to do exactly as you wish. This is just not so.

The important thing is not to get too hung up about copyright issues. All you can do is make lawyers and users of your library and information service aware of the guidelines within which they must operate.

(As this book was going to press, the implementation process for the new EU Copyright Directive (2001/29/EC) was underway in the UK. Readers are therefore advised to contact any of the organisations mentioned above for guidance as to the current state of law with regard to the photocopying and dissemination of material in law firms.)

Note

1. Taken from the CLA's notice 'Important legal information'.

9

You're on your own now

This chapter is devoted to the special problems and circumstances of being a 'one-man band' or 'solo librarian/ information professional' which can be defined as 'all those librarians, information scientists, and information workers who manage information units on their own, or who work as the solo professional, providing a library and information service with the minimum of support'.[1] You may be the sole information professional in a firm or running a departmental library supporting a specialised practice area in a large firm.

As someone who has spent well over half their information career as a 'one-man band', I can vouch for the fact that it can be an enjoyable as well as a frustrating role – enjoyable because you can run things just the way you want but frustrating in the sense that you are 'firefighting', merely being reactive and responding to everyday requests with little opportunity for developing the service and injecting new ideas.

Many, if not all, the ideas and suggestions raised in this chapter can be applied to any information professional at whatever level in whatever role. Some, of course, are more relevant to the role of someone working on their own, but all can be applied as best practice in any circumstance.

You and your surroundings

If it is 'just you', then you will undertake a wide range of information roles. This may include managing a budget, dealing with enquiries, ordering books, training users, shelving books, updating loose-leaf encyclopaedias, circulating journals, providing a current awareness service – in fact, the whole range of tasks from the complex to the mundane.

A solo information professional may have an assistant in a full- or part-time post usually designated as 'non-professional', though it is invidious to make such distinctions – when there are two of you the professional and non-professional roles do become blurred. If you do find yourself in a job where you are completely on your own, it is worth asking your employers, or the person you report to, whether you can call on the services of a secretary or administrative assistant attached to another lawyer or department for occasional help with such tasks as shelving, loose-leaf filing or taking telephone calls during your absence.

If no internal assistance is available, it may be worth considering buying in help on an ad hoc basis or perhaps for a special project. Such a step will obviously have an impact on your budget as well as the firm's policy with regard to outsourcing.

If you want to be seen as an information *professional*, then you must ensure that both you and your environment present a professional image. You must be dressed smartly, even if your firm operates a 'dress down' policy. Ensure that your office or library space is well organised with clear labelling and signing so that users can find what they want (remember, many lawyers work long hours and you are not always going to be there to assist them, so make sure they can locate material easily).

If you have an issue system, whether it is of the electronic variety or the more basic 'signing out' type, then make sure users know how to use it.

If you have a walk-up PC (i.e. a stand-alone PC) in the library, make sure that its positioning meets all requirements regarding health and safety. Is the chair in front of the PC adjustable so that different users can fix it at the right level to ensure that their eyeline roughly corresponds with the top of the PC? If users can access a CD or database on this PC, are straightforward guidance notes on how to use the systems close at hand? Is any dedicated study area well lit and the chairs comfortable and suitable? Are the shelves tidy with journals and newspapers stored away?

The one thing you must try and avoid is clutter. Nothing gives off a worse impression than entering an information department and seeing piles of papers and books on the floor. Besides looking unprofessional, these piles are a health and safety hazard. If you have limited shelf space and find your stock is expanding rapidly, then you must either do some serious weeding, investigate off-site storage or ask if there is any shelf space elsewhere in the firm where items can be stored, although my experience of law firms is that shelf space is always at a premium. And finally, take a look at your own desk – is your in-tray overflowing? are there piles of papers that need sorting out?

I do not want to labour the point too much and some readers may think I am placing too much emphasis on what they may see as such superficial concerns as 'image' and the 'look' of your office, but I believe it is important to be aware of your surroundings and what they say about you and the attitude you have to your job and your place in the firm. The firm's partners often bring visitors and clients to see the library or information department and first impressions do count.

Self-management and motivation

As a solo information professional, it is essential that you learn the art of managing yourself and your time.

Maintain a 'things to do' list and tick off each task as it is completed. Regularly monitor and revise the list to ensure that the important jobs such as dealing with enquiries are done first. It is helpful to plan your day; if you have to input items into a database or catalogue material, make sure you set yourself a target of doing a certain number each day. Assess those times of the day when you are feeling at your freshest – some people are at their best in the morning, others get into their stride later in the day – and make use of this 'premium' time to do those jobs that you find difficult. It could be inputting a rather complex piece of know-how, or telephoning someone whom you think may be able to assist you with a tricky enquiry.

The best laid plans...

You have compiled your 'things to do list', planned your day, timetabled your difficult jobs for that hour just before lunch, the time of the day when you know that you are likely to be firing on all cylinders, and it all goes pear-shaped the moment you walk in the office. You receive a telephone call from a lawyer saying they are having a meeting with a new client in an hour's time and could you, as a matter of urgency, dig up any information you can find on them.

This is where the first lesson for the solo information professional kicks in – being flexible and having the ability to prioritise. In other words, yes, draw up a daily work plan, but allow for the fact that things will crop up to disrupt that plan.

Handling enquiries

How an information professional deals with the enquiries that comes his way is the one factor that usually determines how his information service will be judged. However tidy the shelves are, whether the backlog of know-how has been cleared and inputted, all will pale into insignificance beside the fact that if enquiries are not dealt with satisfactorily, the service will get a bad reputation.

The level of enquiries is usually driven by the amount of work coming into the firm or practice area. If a big deal is underway, you may find that the whole of your day is taken up with enquiries and that essential administrative tasks or necessary items flagged on your daily 'to do' list are being neglected. It is essential therefore to prioritise the type of enquiries you get. Not every one is desperately urgent (whatever the lawyer might say). Obviously, as in the example noted above, if someone is going into a meeting in an hour's time for which he needs some back-up information, you must drop what you are doing and devote your attention to finding that information. If you are asked to provide some research assistance for an article a lawyer is writing whose publication deadline is in a month's time, then you could put off starting work on it for a day or two. In most firms, a partner's demand for information will usually take precedence over that of a trainee solicitor. An essential part of a trainee solicitor's role is research and the information officer's role in this instance would very much be one of providing assistance and guidance on sources.

If you are an information officer attached to a specialised practice area within a large corporate firm and receive an enquiry from a lawyer outside your own practice area, you need justifiably only provide the minimum of assistance or contact their own dedicated information officer and just point them in the right direction regarding sources of information.

Essential administration

Always try and do one of your essential 'back-room' or administrative tasks (e.g. inputting data) each day to avoid backlogs building up. If you have had a day where there has been a constant stream of enquiries with no chance of completing one of these administrative tasks, then carry that task over to the next day and do it first thing (before the next enquiry comes up!). This kind of prioritising comes with practice as confidence in your role develops. The art of maintaining several balls in the air at one time in the manner of a skilful juggler is a major part of being a solo information professional and if you are the kind of person who can really only focus on one task at a time, then 'one-man band' work is probably not for you.

Meetings

From time to time, you will be called upon to attend an internal meeting, maybe with your managing partner to discuss the firm's information strategy or with representatives from the IT department to discuss the development of a new database. When you are a busy solo information professional working on an urgent enquiry and the time of the meeting is looming, the temptation is to cancel the meeting and concentrate on the day-to-day work. This temptation is to be resisted! It is all too easy to cancel a meeting in such circumstances but this is a short-term view. Meetings often focus on long-term developments and policies regarding your department and if you are not there to put forward your point of view, you can hardly complain if decisions are made in your absence that you are subsequently unhappy with.

The paper mountain

Dealing with the paper mountain

For every piece of paper of whatever type that passes across your desk, deal with it by employing one of the 'three Ds':

- Do it.
- Delegate it.
- Dump it.

Do it

Take immediate action on it. Do it now, get it done and out of the way. Order that book, look up that statistic, photocopy that case.

Putting aside a piece of work to be actioned later can be included under this section. It could be a note to yourself to check out a new website or a piece of in-depth research that requires some planning on your part before getting it under way. It could be advance notice of a new book from a publisher that you need to look at more carefully before making a purchasing decision. However, do not let that pile of work 'to be actioned later' get out of hand and become the 'pile of work you are never going to get round to dealing with'. Add the date of receipt to each piece of work you get to serve as a reminder to yourself of how long it has been lying on your desk and, in addition, add each piece of work to your daily list of 'things to do'.

There will come a point when work in this pile is just never going to get done as yet more urgent work comes your way each day. I hope that if the pile has included enquiries or invoices to be paid that these have been dealt with, but there may be other work in this 'to do later' pile that does not have the same weight or urgency (checking out that new website mentioned above is a good example) and that you just never seem to get round to dealing with. If the piece of work has been dated two, three or even six months ago and it still has not been actioned, then the likelihood of its ever being actioned is remote. The time has now come to move it into the third of the three 'D' categories and 'dump it'. If it is that important, it will turn up again, I can guarantee it.

Delegate it

Pass the work on to someone else to action. If you have an assistant then delegation should not be a problem, but many solo information professionals do find delegating difficult. They feel that only they can do the particular job in hand to a standard that satisfies them. Delegating successfully is an art – the following tips may help in becoming a successful delegator:

- You must be able to 'let go' – you cannot be expected to do everything. Why create unnecessarily heavy workloads for yourself and the consequent stress arising from that heavy workload when you can pass it on to someone else?

- Do not be so arrogant as to assume that only you can do everything properly.

- When passing on a piece of work to a colleague, explain clearly what needs to be done and the timeframe in which it is to be completed.

- Make sure you explain the background to the task in hand, particularly if you are passing on a job that has already been partly done and needs completing. There is nothing more frustrating for a colleague than undertaking a job or task 'in limbo' and being unaware of the context and background of what they are being asked to do.

- Do not just delegate the routine or less than interesting work.

- Make your assistant feel involved in the work of the department and that they are part of a team. After all, they may well be running the department in your absence. For example, if you have attended a meeting where the purchase of a new database was discussed, report back on the meeting to your assistant.

- Give your assistant responsibility for a particular section of the library stock and all the tasks and routines associated with that particular section. For example, if you were to put them in charge of the journals they would ensure that they were kept in good order, chase missing numbers, renew subscriptions, send copies to be bound, photocopy articles and maintain circulation lists.

- Your assistant may not do things exactly the way you would do them but the same result will have been achieved anyway. You must be prepared for this eventuality and accept it.

Delegating is difficult when you are a true solo operator (i.e. when you do not have any assistance at all even on a shared or part-time basis). However, there are still ways in which it can be done: that invoice the publisher is chasing payment for can be passed to the accounts department or that tricky enquiry can be passed on to an external research consultancy that charges for its services.[2] Requests for photocopies of journal articles can be passed on to the lawyer's secretary or a central print room or photocopying facility if the firm has one.

Dump it

The ultimate filing system of them all: WPB (waste paper bin). Be ruthless! If the publisher's flyer is advertising a book that is way outside your budget, bin the leaflet. You still have not had time to check the suitability of that freebie journal that arrived in your office two months ago, so bin it. It is more than likely that the publishers will send you another free copy in a few months time, or one of the lawyers may draw your attention to it, and by so doing, give the task of assessing its content and viability for your department more importance.

Reducing the paper mountain

In these days of instant electronic communication and susbscriber lists being passed on to other parties, it is inevitable that your name will be forwarded to suppliers and, before you know it, you are receiving all kinds of unsolicited mail, both e-mail and snail mail. In the early days of being in a new post and particularly if you are working in an area of law with which you are unfamiliar, these flyers can be useful as they enable you to get to know what is available in your topic area and who the main publishers are. You just never know what your attention may be drawn to with unsolicited mail – you may come across an answer to a question that has been bothering you for some time or discover an expert in your field that you were previously unaware of. However, there may come a point when you feel you are overwhelmed with all the unsolicited paper that is landing on your desk. You will need to balance the time and effort in contacting suppliers and publishers to ask them to remove you from mailing lists with the ease of throwing the paper away. And, of course, you may just be missing that vital new publication which will make your life as a solo information professional that much easier.

(I realise of course that you are likely to have built up a relationship with a publisher or book supplier who will normally meet all your requirements regarding the purchasing of books, but there is still room for serendipity.)

It is not just paper crossing your desk that must be dealt with. There are two other forms of communication which will intrude on your daily work routine, so the following sections are devoted to managing telephone calls and e-mails.

The telephone

People use the telephone usually when they require a quick answer to a question. If your firm does not have e-mail, then the telephone will probably be the major form of communication. It is difficult to ignore the insistent ringing of a telephone but there will be occasions when you need to concentrate on a difficult task and would prefer not to answer it. If you have an assistant or a secretary then calls can be forwarded to him or her, but if you are truly a solo information professional, you may be able to ask the switchboard to take messages for you.

If you use one of the modern 'all singing all dancing' telephones where you can key in messages such as 'In a meeting' or 'At lunch' then you have a very effective way of controlling incoming calls literally at your fingertips. Voicemail or a telephone answering machine is another excellent way of managing telephone calls, but remember to change your message when you are back in the office or as your working circumstances dictate.

Tips for reluctant telephone users

If you do have to make a potentially difficult telephone call (e.g. telling that pushy sales rep that you do not want to subscribe to their wonderful new database) then the following tips may help make things go smoothly:

- Only make the call when you are feeling at your best; do not telephone them when you are feeling run down and tired.

- 'Psych' yourself up – rehearse what you are going to say by running the conversation through your head. Try and anticipate any objections or comments the other person might raise and have your responses ready.

- If the other person is not available, leave a message asking them to ring you back later. At the least, it will give you a bit more time to plan your conversational strategy! If they do not return your call within a reasonable time period, telephone them again.

- Stand up when you make the call – it can be very empowering and make you feel in control of the situation.

- Whatever you do, do not lose your temper. If the other person becomes abusive, take charge of the situation and state that you are terminating the call and will ring them back later to resume the conversation by which time it is more than likely they will have calmed down and be more reasonable.

E-mail

In the offices where it is available, most business people now receive more e-mails than telephone calls. E-mail does have many attractions: it is a boon for the reluctant telephone user who finds it easier to compose a quick message and communication with people across different time zones has been transformed.

There is a temptation to regard all e-mail messages as urgent but this must be resisted. Some certainly will be but in my experience most are not. The 'three Ds' policy described above can be applied to managing your e-mail messages: in other words, 'do' by dealing with the message straightaway, 'delegate' by storing the message in a 'folder' or printing it off to be dealt with later, or 'dump' by deleting it.

It is important to create folders in which to store messages that you would like to archive; do not let your inbox become unwieldy, keep it manageable; regularly clear messages in your sent folder or set up an autoarchive option.

The following tips may assist in controlling the number of e-mails appearing in your inbox:

- Be selective in the number of news alerter services you sign up to.

- Turn off your e-mail during busy periods and create an out-of-office auto responder message to indicate to people sending you messages that you are not immediately available to deal with them. Do, however, try to resist putting up the message 'In a meeting' too often. 'In a meeting' must be one of the most overused phrases in business and I would recommend it be used sparingly. If I am inputting know-how I create an auto responder message on the lines of 'I am inputting know-how this afternoon and will not be checking my e-mails regularly. Please telephone me if your enquiry is urgent.'

How to say 'no'

There will be occasions when, because of your heavy workload, you will have to say 'no' to a request for information or assistance.

If lawyers are busy working on deals or have a number of meetings with clients, this usually has an effect on the information officer's workload in that the increased activity is reflected in increased demands on his time.

Never refuse to do something without justification and explanation and certainly not without assessing the circumstances first. For example, if you are asked to photocopy articles from a journal but are working on one enquiry with another two in the pipeline which have deadlines in two hours time, then it is reasonable to ask that a trainee solicitor or secretary does the photocopying.

There can be situations where saying 'no' can have long-term benefits for yourself and your department. Let me explain.

In the following scenario, one of the firm's partners has been given a collection of 25 legal books by a colleague who no longer needs them. The books need to be sorted, catalogued, classified and summaries written of each one's contents for a special bulletin that is to be circulated among the firm's lawyers and it must be completed within ten days.

Your response might be: 'Yes, I will certainly do that.' After the partner has left your office, you realise though that it is rather a lot of books to catalogue, classify and summarise within the stipulated time period. You have had a higher number of enquiries than usual recently and got behind with inputting know-how and this new project is going to set you back even further. On checking your calendar, you notice that the meeting with the partners to discuss the annual library budget is only five days away and you have not yet prepared a draft budget for the forthcoming financial year. You also recall that an important deal is closing in two days time which may well generate some last minute calls for research assistance. The realisation dawns on you that the chances of completing the task in the period agreed upon is going to be impossible to achieve.

What can you do? Speak to the partner and ask if you can request more time to do the task? However, when you do raise the problem with him, he responds by asking why you did not raise the question of the deadline when he first spoke to you. Anyway, he informs you that he has already spoken to his colleague who donated the materials and told him to come in to the office after the ten days to pick up one of the special bulletins and have a look at the collection arranged on the library shelves. If he tells him now that the bulletins will not be ready in ten days time, he says he will 'lose face'.

It looks like you will be working late every night for the next week or so in order to get the task completed on time.

When you were originally asked by the partner to undertake the project, it would have been better if you had taken control of the situation by answering along the lines of:

> 'I can certainly do that but, unfortunately at the moment, my workload is pretty heavy. I have had a higher than usual number of enquiries over the past few days which has meant that I have had to neglect inputting know-how; rather a lot of it has come in since you stressed the need for items to be forwarded to me at the last team meeting. In addition, I have a meeting, as you may recall, with yourself and the other partners on Wednesday to discuss next year's library budget and I must prepare some facts and figures to present at that meeting. Taking all those circumstances into account, ten days time is just too tight a deadline in which to complete such a big project. A more realistic deadline for me would be a month.'

I think any reasonable person would respond positively to such arguments and agree to revise the deadline. However, in this case, the partner says that is very important that the task is done in ten days time but he appreciates your present heavy workload and therefore is going to authorise the employment of a temp to undertake the project under your supervision.

The project is therefore completed within the original stipulated time period; in fact, your temporary member of staff completes it within seven days so you are able to use their three remaining days with you to complete some other tasks which you seem never to have been able to get round to doing.

Saying 'no' for the right reasons is easier to do the longer you have been in a particular post and the better you know the firm's working methods and philosophy.

Isolation

Working as a solo information professional does mean that you can become professionally isolated. You lack the normal day-to-day support of a team of colleagues not just from a purely social point of view (you may be situated in a room on your own) but also on a practical basis, whether it be for assistance with an enquiry or simply to lift your spirits if you are feeling a bit 'down' on that particular day. On the other hand, you are removed from such distractions as office politics and the minutiae of your colleagues' personal lives (unless you choose to get involved in either or both of them, of course).

However, 'no man is an island',[3] and it is important that you do not isolate yourself within your firm, either personally or professionally. Your role must be seen to be as valid and as important as that of the lawyers. The following is a list of tips as an aid against isolation:

- If you are feeling down and overwhelmed with the amount of work you have to do that day, psych yourself up with some appropriate words to exhort yourself to 'get on with it'. I find the website MyNewAttitude.com (*http://www.mynewattitude.com*) useful. Described as 'your home for self help, self improvement [with] ideas & inspiration to change your attitude and change your life' there is usually a short essay or article on the site that helps me face the day with a more positive outlook.

- Get out from behind your desk. Personally deliver the results of a database search to the lawyer who requested it rather than putting it in the internal post.

- Talk to your colleagues at the coffee machine – not just the lawyers but also the secretaries, postmen, print room staff and cleaners.

- Attend any team or group meetings and contribute when necessary.

- Invite colleagues out to lunch.

Networking

It is important for any information professional, but particularly for those who work on their own, to network outside their immediate work environment with colleagues from other law firms and information disciplines. Both CILIP

(Chartered Insitute of Library and Information Professionals) and BIALL (British and Irish Association of Law Librarians) are both good starting points for locating local groups that you can join.

Getting a name for yourself as a helpful contact on an electronic discussion list or by contributing articles to a journal is all well and good, but actual contact with others from your own profession is important for a number of reasons:

- personal and career development;
- getting an insight into how other law firms and the information staff within them operate;
- gaining a wider perspective of the information profession;
- swapping ideas about best practice and procedures;
- meeting people whose subject expertise you may be able to draw on in the future;
- problem solving;
- picking up tips about new databases and useful websites.

Some typical networking opportunities include:

- conferences and seminars;
- courses;
- local branches and groups.

Even in the most structured situation such as attending a course or seminar, there will be opportunities to talk to your fellow attendees during coffee and lunch breaks. If your firm does not have a budget for sending delegates to conferences, there is more than likely to be a local gathering of legal information professionals. The benefits of joining this type of group are enumerated in an article in the February 2003 issue of the *Newsletter of the British and Irish Association of law Librarians*.[4]

Some people are natural networkers, others have to work a bit harder at it. Even those who exude confidence in a business situation can feel ill at ease in a roomful of people. The trick is to 'act as if' you are confident (even if you are not!) or 'fake it until you make it'.

- Do not gravitate towards those people you already know.
- Before you attend the meeting, make a mental note to speak to at least, say, three people.
- Have a business card ready to hand out. (If your firm has not provided them, sets of business cards can be printed at a number of high-street outlets.)
- Follow up new contacts with an e-mail message or telephone call.

At the end of a busy working day, it does sometimes require effort to attend another meeting in the evening, but the importance of networking should not be underestimated.

Conclusion

The perception of the solo information professional by other practitioners in the information world is that it is often a role in which you are merely being reactive, that is you are responding to requests from users and there are few opportunities to be 'proactive', to add value to your service, to initiate ideas and projects and to develop the service you provide.

There is an element of truth in this and much will depend on the circumstances of the job, how busy you generally are and whether you have an assistant. It has to be said though that in many solo information posts, those aspects of the information professional's role that do 'add value' to a firm's library and information service, such as training and current awareness, have to go by the board as the reality of just keeping things ticking over must take precedence.

Having said that, the role of the solo legal information officer can be a very rewarding one. A capable information professional who involves himself in the work of the firm or department to which he is attached can quickly become a highly regarded and valued member of the team.

Notes

1. Sue Lacey Bryant (1995) *Personal Professional Development and the Solo Librarian* (Library Training Guide). Library Association Publishing.
2. I am thinking of services like the FT Business Research Service. Many of the larger UK public libraries also now have paid-for business information services.
3. John Donne: Meditation XVII.
4. Mary Booth (2003) 'Business librarian in London to freelance law librarian in Manchester', *Newsletter of the British and Irish Association of Law Librarians*, February, pp. 14–15.

10

The future for the legal information professional

Sue Hill, of Sue Hill Recruitment, said at the end of 2001 that 'legal information recruitment has been one of our strongest growth areas over the last eighteen months and ... despite the promised recession, it shows no sign of slowing down.'[1] This all sounds good news for both the established legal information professional as well as those considering becoming one. But, in reality, the picture is not so rosy. There is a threat to the traditional information professional from the disillusioned and dissatisfied lawyer and from those seeking a career in which they can utilise their legal qualifications and skills.

In the UK, there are 85,300 solicitors compared to 23,000 members of CILIP.[2] There are 12,000 law graduates each year of whom only 5,000 obtain training contracts with law firms.[3] A survey of junior lawyers in City firms, undertaken by the City of London Law Society (CILS) and *Legal Week* in late 2002, found that 31 per cent of those who responded wanted to quit the profession.[4] What happens to all these surplus law graduates and dissatisfied lawyers? Many of them end up doing legal information work.

Anecdotal evidence suggests that employers prefer their legal information staff to have first a legal background and then an information background; many are quite happy to employ someone in an information post who has just the requisite legal qualifications with no information qualifications whatsoever. In the big City of London law firms, which is the type of law firm that I am most familiar with, the library and information staff are a mixture of the following:

- non-law graduates who have completed a postgraduate diploma in information studies;

- non-law graduates who have completed a postgraduate diploma in information studies and are pursuing the route to chartership or who are already chartered;

- law graduates who, for whatever reasons, have decided not to become lawyers and have moved over into information work. Some may eventually do a postgraduate qualification in information studies and then gain their chartership, others may not. In my experience, most do not obtain any information qualifications at all;

- practising lawyers who have decided, for whatever reasons, to cease practising law and have moved over into information work. Some may do a postgraduate qualification in information studies and then gain their chartership, others may not. In my experience, most do not obtain any information qualifications at all.

In an article on the divide between qualified and non-qualified information personnel in the legal information world, Meredith Gibson said: 'The lack of insistence on a professional qualification in information has contributed to the view held by many, *but in my experience particularly by lawyers* [my italics], that anyone with a degree and a modicum of sense can run an information service.'[5]

Why do lawyers and those who recruit legal information staff put information skills second to legal skills? Their argument is that someone supporting lawyers in an information capacity needs to have a knowledge of the law in order to provide a satisfactory service and do the job properly. They do not seem to appreciate that a non-legally qualified person can pick up enough legal knowledge on the job and off the job by reading and attending courses to fill in the gaps in their knowledge. After all, as an information officer is not providing advice to clients, he does not need to have the depth and extent of legal knowledge that a practising lawyer must necessarily have.

There is also the question of the stereotypical image of the 'librarian' that still persists in the minds of many lawyers, i.e. the lack of drive, absence of business acumen and poor communication skills. In an article on legal recruitment Sue Hill recounts how one HR person in a law firm 'looked rather embarrassed when trying to explain to us that they didn't want a *typical librarian* [my italics] although the person they were seeking should have *some* [my italics] librarian skills'.[6]

Librarian vs lawyer

The one area where information professionals do have the advantage over lawyers is in their knowledge of classification, taxonomies, thesauri and indexing. But even here, we are being challenged by those in the information profession who question the need for information professionals to actually possess any classification skills at all.

> The increasing amount of information available via electronic sources and the existence of 'intelligent' search systems... has helped to spark continuing debate about whether the traditional cataloguing and classification skills of the information professional are becoming increasingly redundant.[7]

A survey of the usefulness of cataloguing and classification (cat 'n' class) skills to new legal information professionals found that 'there was a general feeling that any cataloguing and classification skills which were being used [in the workplace] had not been learnt on the information studies course'.[8] Here we have the teachers of future information professionals playing into the hands of the lawyers who believe that such skills can be learned on the job.

And yet there is evidence to prove that where lawyers have created classification schemes the end result has not been successful. The same survey referred to one firm whose know-how system was maintained by professional support lawyers with no background in information management. 'The result was a database from which neither the lawyers nor the information professionals could easily find information and a new full-text know-how database was being planned which was to be developed by the information professionals using their information management skills.'[9]

It's all on their desktop

There is another area where the need to have qualified information professionals in law firms has been questioned and that concerns the availability of data on lawyers' desktop PCs. Typically, this will consist of databases which have been designed specifically to facilitate searching by the end user. Allied to this is the widespread belief that everything is on the Internet. Who needs an information professional to act as an intermediary when lawyers can find what they want for themselves?

But can they? There have been many occasions in my current post when lawyers have come to me and said they have spent time searching a database or the Internet for a piece of information and been unable to find what they wanted. Only days before writing this particular chapter a partner told me that he had unsuccessfully tried to locate a report on the Internet the previous evening after I had left the office. Within five minutes, I had located the required report and printed it off for him.

Setting aside the fact that some law firms do not make databases available on lawyers' PCs anyway, there are a number of reasons why lawyers are not suited for the role of end user:

- They may not be frequent users of the system and have forgotten any training they may have had and be unable to navigate the system.

- They may not understand such concepts as Boolean searching.

- Their time is expensive: why should a lawyer whose charge-out fees may be £250 per hour spend valuable time searching the Internet when an information professional can do it for him at a fraction of the cost and time involved?

- Despite the best endeavours of those who design and maintain intranets, they can be confusing and difficult for the user to find his way around.

- However often a database is updated, there will always be the case that was heard yesterday or the old piece of legislation that does not get loaded on a database.

- They cannot be expected to know all the search terms unique to each database. For example, one database may use the exclamation mark (!) to indicate truncation, another the asterisk (*).

- They may be unaware of the range of search engines available for searching the Internet and how each one has its own particular strengths and weaknesses.

- They will be unaware of alternative ways of finding the information they want. If they have been unable to find the material on the database they have searched, they may well assume that the information is not available anywhere else. Alternatively, of course, they may just not have done the search properly.

- Many older lawyers are resistant to technology and require assistance in locating material.

The onward march of the professional support lawyer

The biggest threat to the traditional information professional in law firms comes from the professional support lawyer (PSL), sometimes referred to as a professional development lawyer (PDL), but the former term is the one most in use.

It has been estimated that in 2001 there were 300–400 PSLs employed in law firms.[10] PSLs are qualified lawyers who, for whatever reasons, have chosen to give up fee-earning work and taken on a support role which can include the following types of work (this list is derived from personal knowledge as well as the literature on the role of the PSL):

- drafting standard documentation or templates;
- assisting and advising the firm's fee-earning lawyers;
- internal training and education, arranging conferences and seminars, giving presentations on legal practice;
- writing journal articles;
- collecting know-how from lawyers and summarising its content;
- dissemination of internal information;
- developing the library and information service;
- marketing and promoting the firm or the practice area to which they are attached.

It will be noted that many of these areas encroach on the information professional's territory.

Certainly, the information professional can assist lawyers with their research enquiries and advise them on the best sources to use, but he cannot 'advise' in the sense that PSLs can and here I use the word 'advise' deliberately. An information professional can present a lawyer with a section of a statute but cannot *advise* that lawyer whether it would be suitable to apply it in a particular context. The PSL can, of course, because he has been a practising lawyer and is able to apply the law in practical working situations. Here then is the fundamental difference in the way that the PSL and the information professional deal with 'information'. The PSL is taking the raw information or data one step further than the information professional can (even if that information professional has a legal qualification) simply because he is a *qualified lawyer*.

Collecting know-how from lawyers and summarising its content is a role that many information professionals in law firms undertake; if they do not have legal qualifications or training, they may find some of the concepts and terminology difficult to understand which may lead to a contents summary which is inaccurate and misleading. It makes sense, therefore, for a PSL to undertake this role. In some law firms, the PSL prepares the summary and then hands it over to the information officer for inputting. The distinction between these two functions will not be lost on readers, I am sure.

PSLs make it to the top in information management posts too. It is not unusual to find every information post at director level in a City law firm being held by a lawyer, or that all the major initiatives relating to the development of information provision and delivery driven by a mixture of lawyers and IT specialists.

Why are information professionals not getting involved in these initiatives or obtaining these director level posts? It is not just distrust of the information professional by senior partners, as discussed earlier. I think part of the answer lies with the nature of the information professional himself. While there are many focused, savvy, driven, business-like individuals in the legal information world, many do lack that extra drive or ambition to get them to the top. I have spoken to many information professionals over the years and often ask what prompted them to enter the profession. In virtually every case, the answer was that they could not think of anything else they wanted to do or that they drifted into it – hardly the words of people with a determination to get to the top of their profession.

Working with PSLs

PSLs and information professionals have complementary skills and the two working together can deliver a high-quality service to the firm or department in which they operate. Put simplistically, the information professional can draw on the PSL's legal knowledge and the PSL can draw on his colleague's information management skills. There will be differences in their respective disciplines and backgrounds which will make for a useful exchange of ideas and experience. One of the PSLs I work with remarked that once she started summarising know-how for our internal database, she had to rethink the way she had been taught to express herself as a lawyer, i.e. instead of being precise in the terminology used when drafting legal documents, she now had to think of alternative terms and keywords in order that the item could be retrieved by someone searching for it. In other words, she had to start thinking like an information professional.

Some PSLs, however, do not want to align themselves too closely with their information colleagues. There is the perception in some law firms that the PSL is a second-class citizen, the argument being that if they cannot hack it as a fee-earning lawyer, they take the easy option of becoming a support lawyer. If a PSL already has to fight this prejudice, they do not want the additional one of being seen as anything to do with information staff who are often perceived as being of an even lower status.

In my experience, PSLs see themselves first and foremost as lawyers and not as information practitioners even though their particular role in the firm may largely consist of information-related functions.

For the medium or small-sized firm, a PSL in a library and information function can be a very attractive proposition from an employer's point of view, as it solves the firm's information requirements at a stroke. The firm has a qualified lawyer who can 'add on' the information skills learned on the job or by reading articles and books.

There is one particular area where information professionals, compared to lawyers, are a very attractive proposition to employers, and that is cost. The stark truth is that information professionals are cheaper than lawyers. The arguments about the low pay of information professionals have been raging for many years and will, no doubt, continue to do so. Even when lawyers move over into information work, although they may not always be paid at the same level as a fee-earning lawyer, they can still earn well in excess of what an information professional would get for the equivalent post. On the other hand, information professionals in the legal sector compared to their information colleagues in other sectors are well paid.

One of the reasons why information professionals can be poorly paid and have low status compared to other professions is that they do not have the unique hard skills of, for example, the accountant, IT specialist, plumber, electrician or lawyer. Information professionals have a portfolio of soft skills drawn from different disciplines which are arguably aptitudes rather than anything that can be learned. A former colleague of mine made this point succintly in an article he wrote for *Business Information Review* when he commented that 'basic library skills are really the specific application of good business practice'.[11]

You are either a service-oriented person or you are not. Those who have chosen to be information professionals are more likely to be service oriented than those who do not choose to become one. Historically, service professions have been poorly paid. Ergo, information professionals are poorly paid.

Career paths

It might be useful at this point to compare the various career paths that a lawyer and an information professional might pursue.

Information professionals

There are three sectors in which information professionals can find employment: public, academic and special. Public refers to libraries maintained by local authorities; academic is a library or information service found in any kind of educational establishment; special is any library which does not fall into either of the other two categories. They include commercial firms (e.g. law firms, accountants, engineers), organisations serving the particular needs of professions (e.g. the Law Society, the Royal Institution of Chartered Surveyors), companies and charities.

Many information professionals remain in the same sector throughout their career, but some do make cross-sector moves, particularly from the public and academic into the special, frankly because the salaries and conditions on offer are often superior. Such moves are usually made within five years of joining the profession; it seems to be more difficult to make such a move the longer you stay in one particular sector.

Despite the frequent references in the literature on job hunting in the information world and the assurances by recruitment consultants that skills and experience are transferable, this is not always so. Once you are in a particular part of the special or commercial sector, it can be very difficult to make the move into another specialisation *within* that sector, for example to move from an accountancy practice to a law firm.

In my experience, recruitment consultants are reluctant to put you forward for posts outside the specialised area in which you have built up your experience because the employer wants someone who can 'hit the ground running' and does not want an employee who will be on a steep learning curve. Recruitment consultants very much like to pigeon-hole candidates: if you have been successful in one area, their argument is that you should build on your strengths by taking another job in the same sector. Presumably, this is what the employer wants too as he has instructed the agency as to the kind of candidate he requires and will be paying the agency's fees once a candidate has been appointed. The agency cannot, therefore, afford to take any risks on a candidate who does not fit the bill. This attitude also confirms what I have said previously in this chapter about managers in law firms preferring legal knowledge and experience over and above information knowledge and experience.

It is difficult then, but not impossible, to move into another subject sector within the commercial information field and you may have to take a cut in salary because, in effect, you are starting at the bottom rung of the ladder in the new sector area as you do not have the required *subject* knowledge.

Lawyers

Upon qualification, lawyers must choose the area of legal specialisation in which they wish to practise. In certain circumstances, this has been determined for them by the type of firm or organisation in which they have done their training. In the bigger law firms, the choice is, theoretically, wider though it will depend on the vacancies available at the time of qualification. Lawyers have told me that it is difficult to change legal specialisation once you have two years PQE (post-qualification experience) behind you.

However, for the lawyer who no longer wishes to *practise* law, there are a number of viable alternative careers open to him (which require no additional qualifications on his part) and these include:

- information management;
- professional support lawyer;
- lecturing;

- journalism;

- training and education.

Of course, an information professional can move into journalism, lecturing and training and also qualify as a lawyer, a process which, including a two-year training contract and part-time study, can take up to six years. By contrast, the qualified lawyer can move straight over into information work without the need to do any kind of information management qualification because, as has been demonstrated above, it is not required or deemed to be necessary.

IT personnel getting in on the act

It is not just lawyers who have hi-jacked traditional library and information roles – the IT specialists are doing it too. Database and intranet development are being undertaken by IT personnel rather than information staff even though web design and database construction employ traditional 'library' skills such as indexing and classification.

Summary

To sum up, these are the areas where the information officer demonstrably has the competitive advantage over the lawyer:

- ability to search a wide range of databases;

- knowledge of different types of web search engine;

- cataloguing and classification, indexing, thesaurus construction;

- compiling bibliographies;

- awareness and knowledge of a wide range of sources (both legal and, more importantly, non-legal);
- database/intranet design and construction;
- cheaper than a lawyer;
- a lateral thinker;
- while the lawyer might be able to search some databases, this frees up the information officer to do the more complex and challenging enquiries.

Conclusion

The truth of the situation is that a lot of people are now entering the legal information profession with skills and experience that are valued by employers over and above those that the traditional graduate entrant to the profession (who has probably done an arts degree topped up with a postgraduate diploma in information studies) can offer.

The trend to me is clear: law firms prefer legal knowledge first and information skills second. The lawyer who subsequently obtains a postgraduate qualification in information studies followed possibly by becoming a chartered member of CILIP has a powerful combination of qualifications that will be very attractive to a potential employer.

I hope that anyone reading this who is considering a career in legal information will not be discouraged by what I have said in this chapter. I have worked in legal information for over five years and it has been the most rewarding and stimulating job of my information career so far. I would also advise any wannabe legal information professional to seek out a wonderful article from the *Law Library Journal* in which 'experienced law librarians explain how at midcareer they continue to find challenges in their jobs and enthusiasm for their work'.[12]

But I would urge anyone who is reading this at college or university and contemplating a career in legal information to consider the options available to him. It is worth bearing in mind that law is an information-rich discipline full of research opportunities; if you are particularly attracted to that aspect of traditional library and information work, then you should perhaps think about qualifying as a lawyer first and an information officer second.

Just before finalising this chapter in March 2003, I was looking at TFPL's website (*http://www.tfpl.com*). TFPL is one of the leading recruitment consultants for the information sector and there, in its list of job vacancies, was a post for a PSL. This was the first time I had seen a PSL post advertised through an information recruitment agency and I am sure it will not be the last.

Notes

1. Sue Hill (2001/2) 'Earnest of success', *Legal Information Management*, 1(4), Winter 3–5.
2. Tim Owen (2002) 'All change? Reskilling for the 21st century', *Legal Information Management*, 2(4) Winter, 4–7.
3. 'Law firms snubbing "new" universities', 7 November 2002 (*http://www.news.bbc.co.uk/1/hi/education/2418013.stm*), accessed 30 March 2003.
4. 'City assistants blighted by stress', *Legal Week*, 7 November 2002, p. 1.
5. Meredith Gibson (2001) 'Telling it like it is: a personal take on information', *Business Information Review*, 18(1), 28–34.
6. Hill (2001/2) 'Earnest of success'.

7. Gillian Sands (2002) 'Cat and class: what use are these skills to the new legal information professional?', *Legal Information Management*, 2(2), Summer, 19–22.

8. Ibid.

9. Ibid.

10. Chris Muir (2002) 'Professional development lawyer: where do we go from here?', *PLC*, XIII (8), September 94–6.

11. Steve Borley (1999) 'Shortcut to the skills base: the case for non-library school trained information staff', *Business Information Review*, 16(4), December, 192–6.

12. 'Care and maintenance of the successful career: how experienced law librarians make their work rewarding', *Law Library Journal*, 93(4), Fall 2001, 535–87.

Appendix 1
A week in the life of a legal information officer

The following diary is intended to give a flavour of what day-to-day life in a law firm is like for a legal information officer. I have tried to include most of what happened over a five-day period including the minutiae of everyday office life, but have had to be less than specific about the subject matter of some of the enquiries I received for reasons of confidentiality.

The diary was compiled over five consecutive days in April 2003.

I support sixty lawyers (partners, assistants and trainees) specialising in funds and insurance regulation (the 'practice area' or 'the group').

Day 1

09.15 Into the office to find the proceedings of a conference on exchange traded funds that a lawyer has left on my desk. I decide to input details into the know-how system straightaway. This takes some time as there are about twenty papers that need summarising. This is a useful piece of know-how as conference proceedings often represent current thinking on a particular topic.

10.05 Coffee break. I then decide to devote the rest of the morning to researching the sources of information on a particular topic in which a partner is interested and where the firm hopes to develop business.

11.29 A secondee who has returned from a six-month stint in Switzerland asks me whether during his absence there have been any updates to certain publications that lawyers in the group receive. I ask him to send me an e-mail detailing which particular ones he has and I will look into it.

13.30 Gently remind (by e-mail) my colleague who deals with EU information that she was going to check a certain point concerning EU law with one of the lawyers in her group. She gets back to me within ten minutes with the answer which I relay to my lawyer who asked the question in the first place. (This enquiry came up before the commencement of the diary and I had done some extensive research on the Europa website (*http://europa.eu.int*) without getting an answer and concluded that it was one of those enquiries that would be best answered by a practitioner.)

14.00 Late lunch.

15.00 Continue working on this morning's major research project finally reporting my findings by e-mail to the partner concerned.

16.10 Inputting know-how.

17.30 Leave office.

Day 2

09.45 Following on from the secondee's enquiry of Day 1 on updating his publications, I check his e-mail that he sent me to see what particular titles he has and then look out the updates for him and take them round to his office. Have a brief chat with him about his time in Switzerland.

10.03 Continue working on an enquiry which I began before keeping this diary. I am trying to track down an article written by a certain author on a specific subject which I was told was written two or three years ago. An initial extensive search did not throw up any articles which fitted these criteria. I also contacted the organisation where the author works and spoke to someone in their library who provided me with a list of all the articles that the author has written in the last three years. Still drew a blank. The lawyer has now come back to me with the suggestion that the article could have been published more than three years ago. I decide, in view of the generally vague nature of the enquiry, to run a search on a periodicals database and pull up details of *all* articles written by the author. I forward this to the lawyer concerned and ask him to mark any he thinks could be the one he requires.

10.47 A lawyer brings me a photocopy of a review from a journal of a new publication which she thinks would be a useful addition for the library. I quickly look at the subject matter of the book and the price and tell her that I will order it. I was able to make a quick decision because (a) there is no other book currently available on the topic and it fills a gap in my collection, (b) it is competitively priced and (c) the lawyer is a leading expert in her field and her judgement about a book's merits can be relied upon.

11.10 (See entry for 10.03.) The lawyer gets back to me having consulted the list of possible article titles with a request for copies of four of the full-text articles on the list. We have three of them in the firm which I obtain by liaising with colleagues in other practice area information offices where the titles are kept. The fourth has to be ordered from an organisation that supplies photocopies of journal articles at a cost which is agreed with the lawyer concerned and charged to a file number.

13.15 A partner is looking for some commentary on section 75 of the Financial Services Act 1986, a piece of legislation which has been repealed. Fortunately, there is a fair amount of information in the internal know-how system and I look out half a dozen items for him.

13.55 Late lunch with an information colleague from the firm's media law practice area.

15.00 E-mail our central ordering team with details of the book recommended to me earlier (see entry for 10.03). I did not check the details of price, publisher and ISBN from another source as these had been supplied in the review itself and they can be relied upon.

15.30 Into a meeting with colleagues from another practice area information office and from our systems team to evaluate a new database that we are thinking of purchasing in place of one we already have. Very good presentation by two reps from the database providers and we ask lots of pertinent questions about currency, technical specifications and cost.

17.15 The meeting is over and I have a brief chat with my colleagues about what our initial thoughts are. We agree to meet on the following day to formulate our response to their proposals.

17.25 Check my e-mail inbox to ensure that nothing urgent has come in while I have been in the meeting and then leave the office for the day.

Day 3

09.35 Telephone my colleague from yesterday's meeting (see entry for 15.30) and we agree to meet later on at 15.00 for an exchange of views on the merits and otherwise of the new database.

09.45 Type up this diary.

10.31 Receive an e-mail from a partner requesting a copy of a book which is on the library shelves. I take it round to her office and leave it on her desk and on getting back to my own office send her an e-mail confirming that I have done so.

12.30 Pick up my post (internal and external) from the central mail collection point on my floor. One of the items is the book I ordered yesterday (Day 2, 10.03). I send an e-mail to the lawyer notifying her that it has arrived, classify it and put it on one side for when she is next in the office.

13.00 Lunch.

14.00 Read e-mails which have built up in my inbox.

14.33 A lawyer comes in looking for a legal dictionary. While this is available electronically (and I inform him how to access it on the firm's intranet) I have been getting a number of requests for a hard-copy legal dictionary recently so decide it would be worth seeing what is on the market with a view to a possible purchase. I make a note on my 'to do' list to look into this.

15.00 Meeting with colleague to discuss possible purchase of new database (see 09.35 entry this morning). We decide that it has some major advantages over the system we currently have but that we need some assurances from the providers that further enhancements will be put in place before we can consider taking out a subscription. My colleague will relay our views to the two reps we met yesterday.

15.46 Check my loans register to see which books are overdue. Make a note to chase a lawyer in another practice area who has had one of my library books for some time.

16.05 Telephone call from a lawyer who has just gone on secondment to a company in Switzerland asking if I can look out any documentation relating to the terms and conditions for the appointment of a non-executive director. I find a couple of items which I e-mail to her.

16.46 Read an e-mail from a lawyer advising that in honour of his birthday and the sunny weather there are cakes in the kitchen. I do not need to be told twice!

17.11 Telephone a colleague in the Corporate Finance information office to raise one or two questions about a paper from a member of the IT department proposing changes to the look and feel of our internal know-how database.

Day 4

09.15 Into the office and checked e-mails. Nothing requiring immediate action.

09.53 Lawyer comes in to my office collecting money for the Red Cross appeal in Iraq.

10.06 Lawyer pops her head round the door and we have a brief social chat.

10.14 E-mail from a colleague in another of the firm's information offices drawing my attention to a recently published EU Commission paper. Having checked it out, I decide that, as it is not wholly relevant to the kind of work the lawyers in my group do, I shall not bring it to their attention.

10.27 Trainee lawyer comes in with a series of references he has found on the firm's know-how database to look out the original documents from the files.

10.42 Another trainee comes in and asks me questions about the functionality of our know-how system and why some items can be linked electronically and others cannot. I explain the reasons why.

10.50 Yet another trainee comes in asking how a section of a statute comes into force. I explain that it is usually via a Statutory Instrument Commencement Order and, using the appropriate database, show her how to verify the fact.

10.55 Time for a mid-morning break and encounter a colleague from another practice area information office at the coffee machine. Have a brief chat about the state of the information job market.

11.00 Type up this diary for the last day.

12.10 Secretary returns a know-how file that had been borrowed by one of the lawyers.

12.22 Check my current awareness bulletins in my e-mail inbox including one that is forwarded to the lawyers in my group, but decide on this occasion that the contents of today's edition is not relevant, so do not pass it on. Read an e-mail about an upcoming internal lecture on recent developments on contract law which I decide would be worth attending.

12.36 Check my 'to do' list and conclude that as there is nothing urgent to follow up I can clear the papers that have accumulated on my desk over the last week or so.

14.59 Having had lunch and a walk in the warm April sunshine, back to the office to go through some recent know-how that has been donated for the system.

15.16 Urgent telephone call from a lawyer working at home who wants a journals search undertaken on a specific topic. This takes longer than anticipated as my initial search on a legal journals index does not yield as many items as I hoped it would and I have to consult a couple of other sources.

16.37 Afternoon tea.

17.03 The latest *FreePint* newsletter arrives in my e-mail inbox, an invaluable resource for the information professional in any sector. I download it in its PDF format and read it.

17.28 Just thinking about leaving the office and going home when I get a telephone call from a colleague in the Finance information office asking if I have the January 1999 issue of *Institutional Investor* in my journals collection. After checking my files, I telephone to inform her that that particular issue is missing but suggest she may be able to access the article she requires via the appropriate database.

17.31 Telephone call from a lawyer working at home asking if I think, based on my reading of journals and my general awareness of the financial institutions market generally, whether certain terms such as OEICS (open ended investment companies) and ICVC (investment company with variable capital) are in current usage within the industry.

Day 5

09.30 Meeting with Corporate Finance information colleagues to review current trends and exchange news about what is going on in our respective practice area information offices. Meeting broke up at 09.55.

10.16 Meeting with lawyer who is planning to produce bulletins for the group on various aspects of fund management. Based on the types of enquiries I receive, we discuss which subjects she should cover and the best way of marketing and promoting the publications once they have been produced.

10.48 Telephone call from the group's professional support lawyer asking for a progress report on the latest edition of a client bulletin for which I have editorial responsibility.

10.51 Checking e-mails.

11.15 Very interesting enquiry from one of our trainee lawyers concerning a particular section of the Companies Act 1985. He wants to look at any proceedings in Parliament which may have debated the section. We discuss the best way of getting access to this information bearing in mind that, because of the date, it is not going to be available in electronic format. We further discuss how to find out the dates of debates in Parliament and possible local sources where copies of Hansard can be consulted.

11.55 Working on the in-house publication mentioned above.

14.45 Inputting know-how for the rest of the day.

17.45 Leave office.

All in all, a fairly typical week!

Appendix 2
Starting from scratch

This chapter is devoted to the legal information officer who has been tasked with starting up a library and information service in a small or medium-size firm on a very limited budget.

It was only back in 1999 that I went for an interview with a medium-sized law firm in London who did not subscribe to any online databases, did not have access to the Internet and were not using e-mail. They were just about to begin a programme of providing each lawyer with his own desktop PC.

Things have certainly moved on since then in terms of the transmission of information by electronic means in business generally (indeed, I cannot see how even the smallest of businesses these days can survive without having e-mail) but there are still law firms who, because of their size, budget and culture, do not have, or do not wish to have, access to online databases and the Internet, yet require some kind of library and information service.

The Internet

Even if the Internet is not made available generally throughout the firm, I think that as information officer you should make the strongest possible case to the managing partners for you yourself to have access to it. You could point out the wide range of (free) legal websites including the British and Irish Legal Information Institute (BAILII) (*http:// www.bailii.org/*), Legal Resources in the UK and Ireland (*http://www.venables.co.uk/*) and Lawlinks: Legal Information on the Internet (*http://library.kent.ac.uk/ library/lawlinks/default.htm*), as well as the availability of such general information as telephone directories, postcodes, street maps and dictionaries, thus removing the need for spending money on a range of general reference material.

If you have been unsuccessful in persuading the partners of the merits of allowing you to access the Internet, is there an Internet café nearby which you can use or is access available in a public library? The problem with using the Internet in such public environments is that there will be restrictions on time and, more importantly, in view of lengthy statutes devouring reams of paper, on the amount you will be allowed to print. Best go back and have another go at persuading the managing partners you should have access to the Internet at work!

If you have succeeded in getting access to the Internet, sign up for as many free newspaper and news services that you can, e.g. *The Times* (*http://www.timesonline.co.uk/*), *Daily Telegraph* (*http://www.telegraph.co.uk*) and Google news (*http://www.google.co.uk*).

Join some online discussion groups such as Lis-law (*http://www.jiscmail.ac.uk*) or FreePint (*http://www.freepint .com*). These are useful not just for making contacts but they are also invaluable sources of information and advice.

Make use of the British Library Public Catalogue (*http://blpc.bl.uk/*) and any other online catalogues you can locate to check references and the range of titles available for your particular legal specialisation.

If there is a leading publisher covering your area of law who has a website, check it regularly to ensure you keep up to date with what is appearing in your field.

Networking

Join a local information or legal information professional group and attend meetings and events. Both BIALL and CILIP have a network of sub-groups including ones devoted to the needs of solo workers and freelancers.

Make contact with other legal information officers in the region. Look in the telephone directory and make some calls. Visit their libraries, pick up tips and advice, share knowledge.

Book stock

If you have a limited budget which will not stretch to buying both books and loose-leafs, go for the loose-leafs as they are updated regularly.

Open an account with a local bookshop as near to your office as possible in order to ensure speedy delivery for urgent items. You may be entitled to some kind of discount as a business or regular customer.

Keep an eye open, either on the discussion lists you have joined or via the contacts made at the groups you attend, for anyone selling legal texts they no longer require, but bear in mind that out-of-date law books can be a dangerous commodity.

Enquiries

If a local university or college offers law courses, contact the librarian and see if you can use their library to do your legal research.

Investigate the stock of your nearest public library. There may not be a great range of legal texts, but there should be a good reference section and many of the larger libraries offer a business information service which you could make use of (on a paid-for basis).

If you are working in a particular area of the law, contact the professional body that represents that subject (e.g. for property the Royal Institution of Chartered Surveyors, for insurance the Chartered Insurance Institute) and ask what library and information facilities they provide for non-members. Access will probably be restricted to members only but it is more than likely that they will offer some kind of research service, again on a paid-for basis.

Contact the Law Society (*http://www.lawsoc.org.uk/*) and the Institute of Advanced Legal Studies (*http://ials.sas.ac .uk/*) and see what use you can make of their library and information services.

Use your contacts to assist you with urgent requests for case law and articles. I have always found people who work in the information profession ready to assist a colleague in need, but be careful not to presume too much on people's good nature. Always be prepared to return the favour when necessary. If you are constantly being asked for case law from one particular report series, suggest to the managing partners that it would be more cost effective to subscribe to the series rather than pay for one-off photocopies.

As EU (European Union) law impacts on so many areas of English law it is important you familiarise yourself with the Europa (*http://www.europa.eu.int/*) website. This is a site of megalithic proportions so it would be useful to get to know a friendly information officer who specalises in EU matters on whom you can call for guidance and help. The European Information Association (*http://www.eia.org.uk/*) is an excellent gateway into the world of EU information.

You do not always need a vast range of resources to provide an effective information service, just some ingenuity and lateral thinking.

Appendix 3
20 tips for being a first-class legal information officer

How to stay ahead of the rest and ensure your users come back for more, time and time again! In no particular order:

1. Always ensure that every photocopied journal article or section of a book supplied to a lawyer has the full bibliographical details written on the top sheet. You may be surprised to see this item included, but I never cease to be amazed at the number of photocopies I receive from colleagues or come across in files that lack these details, thus rendering them useless.

2. Provide a 'study area' in your library. Most lawyers share offices or sit in open plan arrangements and need somewhere quiet to study documentation or work on complex drafting free from the distraction of office conversations and telephone calls.

3. Provide notices at office photocopiers outlining copyright regulations and what can and cannot be copied.

4. Prepare guides for those databases and CDs that are made available to lawyers on their desktops or for walk-up PCs that may be situated in the library. Confine each guide to one side of an A4 sheet and laminate it in order to prolong its useful life.

5. When writing an abstract, designing a website, putting across your ideas, constructing a classification system, remember KISS – 'Keep It Simple and Straightforward'.

6. Do not give up on an enquiry until you have proved to your own satisfaction that there is not an answer to it.

7. Prepare a list of recommended websites either covering law generally or specific to a particular area of law and distribute a copy to every lawyer in the firm.

8. Sign up for (at least) one e-mail discussion list or join (at least) one work-related professional organisation.

9. Regularly clear out your in-tray and e-mail folders.

10. Spread this message throughout your firm: the Internet does not have the answers to everything.

11. Do not think you need shelves and shelves of books and journals to provide a good library and information service – 80 per cent of enquiries are dealt with by utilising 20 per cent of the stock.

12. Information work is mostly about having the right attitude to your job and your role: if you have an enquiring mind and are responsive to the needs of your users, then everything else will fall into place.

13. Make a note of each lawyers' individual special interests and projects and send them notification of relevant articles/news items/reports as they come to your notice.

14. Delegate whenever you can.

15. Do not become a 'signposting librarian'. If you are asked a question then answer it, do not just point your user in the right direction.

16. Know your information sources as thoroughly as possible.

17. Beware of information overload. Make sure that what you do provide is focused and relevant.

18. Become your firm's web guru. Provide training on searching the Internet. Your stock will rise immediately.

19. Keep the library area tidy and 'professional looking'.

20. Be an active contributing member of your firm or practice area.

Useful contacts

Professional bodies and organisations

Aslib-IMI
Temple Chambers
3–7 Temple Avenue
London EC4Y 0HP
Tel: + 44 (0) 20 7583 8900
Website: *http://www.aslib.com*

A corporate membership organisation publishing books and journals and running training courses, with a recruitment agency and information services.

BIALL (British and Irish Association of Law Librarians)
Website: *http://www.biall.org.uk/home.asp*

An independent and self-supporting body that was created to represent the interests of legal information professionals, documentalists and other suppliers of legal literature and reference materials in the United Kingdom and the Republic of Ireland.

CILIP (The Chartered Institute of Library and Information Professionals)
7 Ridgmount Street
London WC1E 7AE
Tel: + 44 (0) 20 7255 0500
Website: *http://www.cilip.org.uk*

The professional body for librarians, information managers and information scientists, CILIP was formed in 2002 following the merger of the Library Association and the Institute of Information Scientists. Offers training courses, recruitment services, book and journal publications.

City Legal Information Group (CLIG)
Website: *http://www.clig.org/*

CLIG has been organising events on topical issues in legal information provision for the past 26 years. In addition to professional development meetings, CLIG also arranges social events to help information professionals network and share thoughts and experiences.

European Information Association
Central Library
St Peter's Square
Manchester M2 5PD
Tel: +44 (0)161 228 3691
Website: *http://www.eia.org.uk/*

An association of librarians and information officers specialising in European Union material.

Useful websites

All the Web
http://www.alltheweb.com/
Search engine.

BAILII (British and Irish Legal Information Institute)
http://www.bailii.org/
Access to freely available British and Irish public legal information.

BLISS Classification Association
http://www.sid.cam.ac.uk/bca/bcahome.htm

British Library Public Catalogue
http://blpc.bl.uk/

BUBL Information Service
http://www.bubl.co.uk

Copyright Licensing Agency
http://www.cla.co.uk/

Dewey Decimal System
http://www.oclc.org/dewey/

FreePint
http://www.freepint.com
FreePint is a community of information researchers globally.

Google
http://www.google.co.uk/
Search engine.

Institute of Advanced Legal Studies (IALS)
http://ials.sas.ac.uk/

Invisible Web: The Search Engine of Search Engines
http://www.invisibleweb.com/

LawCrawler
http://lawcrawler.findlaw.com
Legal web and databases search.

Lawlinks
http://library.kent.ac.uk/library/lawlinks/default.htm
Legal information on the Internet. An annotated list of websites compiled by Sarah Carter.

Law Society
http://www.lawsoc.org.uk/

Legal resources in the UK and Ireland, maintained by Delia Venables
http://www.venables.co.uk

Lis-law
http://www.jiscmail.ac.uk/lists/lis-law.html
A list for news and discussion on legal information and law libraries.

MyNewAttitude.com

http://www.mynewattitude.com

Self-help, self-improvement, ideas and inspiration.

Newspaper Licensing Agency

http://www.nla.co.uk

SearchEngineWatch.com

http://www.searchenginewatch.com

The source for search engine marketing and optimisation.

Bibliography

Books

Halvorson, T.R. (2000) *Law of the Super Searchers: The Online Secrets of Top Legal Researchers*. CyberAge Books.

Holborn, Guy (2001) *Butterworths Legal Research Guide*, 2nd edn. Butterworths. Designed to guide readers through the difficulties of legal research.

Jeffers, Susan (1991) *Feel the Fear and Do It Anyway: How to Turn Your Fear and Indecision into Confidence and Action*. Arrow Books.

Owen, Tim Buckley (2003) *Success at the Enquiry Desk*, 4th edn. Facet Publishing. Helps the information professional become self-sufficient in answering enquiries.

Pedley, Paul (2000) *Copyright for Library and Information Service Professionals*, 2nd edn. Aslib.

Pedley, Paul (2001) *The Invisible Web: Searching the Hidden Parts of the Internet*. Aslib-IMI.

Yate, Martin John (1992) *Great Answers to Tough Interview Questions: How to Get the Job You Want*, 3rd revised edn. Kogan Page.

Journal articles

Booth, Mary (2003) 'Business librarian in London to freelance law librarian in Manchester', *Newsletter of the British and Irish Association of Law Librarians*, February, p. 14.

Borley, Steve (1999) 'Shortcut to the skills base: the case for the non-library school trained information staff', *Business Information Review*, 16(4), 192–6.

BrightPlanet (2000) 'The Deep Web: Surfacing Hidden Value' (White Paper), *http://www.completeplanet.com/Tutorials/DeepWeb/index.asp*, accessed 12 April 2003.

Brindley, Lynne (2001) 'What use are librarians (working in libraries)?', *Relay*, No. 51.

'Care and maintenance of the successful career: how experienced law librarians make their work rewarding' (2001) *Law Library Journal*, 93(4), 535–87.

'City assistants blighted by stress' (2002) *Legal Week*, 7 November, p. 1.

Edols, Liz (2001) 'Taxonomies are what?', *FreePint*, No. 97, *http://www.freepint.com/issues/041001.htm/feature*, 4 October.

'The future just happened: black holes in cyberspace – the invisible web', *http://news.bbc.co.uk/hi/english/static/in_depth/programmes/2001/future/invisible_web.stm*, accessed 27 January 2003.

Gibson, Meredith (2001) 'Telling it like it is: a personal take on information', *Business Information Review*, 18(1), 28–34.

Hill, Sue (2001) 'Earnest of success', *Legal Information Management*, 1(4), 3–5.

'Law firms snubbing new universities', 7 November 2002, *http://news.bbc.co.uk/1/hi/education/2418013.stm*, accessed 30 March 2003.

Miskin, C. (2002) 'Taxonomies', *Legal Information Management*, 2(1), 16–23.

Muir, Chris (2002) 'Professional development lawyer: where do we go from here?', *PLC*, XIII (8), 94–6.

Owen, Tim (2002) 'All change? Reskilling for the 21st century', *Legal Information Management*, 2(4), 4–7.

Sands, G. (2002) 'Cat and class: what use are these skills to the new legal information professional?', *Legal Information Management*, 2(2), 19–22.

Wilson, T.D. (2002) 'The nonsense of information management', *Information Research*, 8(1), paper no. 144, available at *http://InformationR.net/ir/8-1/paper144.html*.

Index